Unknown Jesus

Unknown Jesus

Jerrod B. McKnight, J.D.

ISBN-13: 9781735871509
Printed in the United States of America

To my beautiful Ashley,
a patient, kind, and loving soul.

I love you!

Contents

Preface

It is not by human faculty alone that I write this book, but by the inspiration of the Holy Spirit. I am simply a sinner that will not be held liable for the debt accrued through sin because of my Savior's grace; I am a man absolutely undeserving of Jesus' unfathomable mercy.

> For the Lord giveth wisdom: out of his mouth cometh knowledge and understanding. He layeth up sound wisdom for the righteous: he is a buckler to them that walk uprightly. He keepeth the paths of judgment, and preserveth the way of his saints. (Proverbs 2:6-8, KJV)

> If any of you lacks wisdom, let him ask of God, who gives to all liberally and without reproach, and it will be given to him. (James 1:5, NKJV)

God is the source of all knowledge; however, He will often use mankind as a relay point to disseminate His knowledge. Many people have served God well in mentoring me to understand sound, Biblical doctrine and theology. In this book,

I provide references where I am certain of the proximate human origin; however, as knowledge has accrued over time, I am regrettably unable to provide references to all sources.

I attribute the inspiration for this book to a thought that the Lord has allowed to grow in my mind over time. My first recollection of this thought dates back approximately ten years to an instance where I was riding through Nashville, Tennessee. On that day, I was a passenger of Wesley Stephens; while my friend drove, we discussed topics ranging from women to softball. For the benefit of his wife, I would like to point out that this conversation predates Lindsey Stephens! As he and I traveled down interstate 40, the conversation turned to God; I made a statement that I really did not fully understand at that point in time. The statement was this: even if God did not do it for anyone else, He became fully human just for me. I was trying to say that I need a God that overcame temptation; One that succeeded while limited in the same manner in which I am limited. If He remained sinless while being tempted like I am tempted, it would prove to me that I can overcome my flesh! At that point in time, I needed victory in my life; God laced my thoughts with a revelation that has become the bedrock of my life. He revealed to me that victory is attainable in my life because it was already achieved just over two thousand years earlier!

This book is the product of approximately ten years of real life. The content of this book is a derivative of what God has done in my life; He called, forgave, saved, guided, trained, and inspired me. Every step I have taken towards God has been enabled and directed by Him. Hate of pride and arrogance is the essence of respect for God (Proverbs 8:13, KJV). This is because God created us, and He holds our future in His hands; our ability, intellect, and health are His alone. My prayer is that the life in these pages will somehow assist each reader as much as it has enabled me. I am not a product of my own devices; I am a result of His mercy, guidance, and provision.

ONE

The Seed of the Woman

The Beginning

Many have mused over the origin of life, the universe, and our environment. Scientists have speculated numerous hypotheses on these topics, most of which can neither be scientifically proven nor disproven. Because of the difficulty in proving or disproving these theories, some have grown in popularity even without definitive proof. Popular theories are fashioned, defended, and disseminated over time, which allow them to become infused into society's belief system, widely accepted, and taught as truth. Some of these commonly accepted theories revolve around how things evolved, were transformed, or exploded into something new. Many Scientists in this field attempt to work backwards chronologically, postulating how matter changed over time in hopes of discovering its origin. However, assuming people can eventually find the point at which matter began, the question still stands: What existed before matter? Some might read this and think: The base substances of matter are the elements on the Periodic Table. Others might read and think: Matter is composed of molecules and atoms. While these are true, we should delve a little deeper by asking ourselves: What existed before the elements on the Periodic Table, and what was the source of atoms? If we truly want to arrive at the source, we should not stop with basic elements, molecules, or atoms! Was there some secret ingredient that changed from its former state into an atom? If so, what existed before this secret ingredient and what existed before that? I hope you are beginning to see the dilemma with which we are faced. If everything came from something then from what was the first something derived? Can something ever be derived from nothing?

You see, even if humans are able to trace all the way back to the point where the first atom began to exist, we are still left with one question: How did something *begin* to exist out of nothing? Can you image trying to make a car when you have no parts and no tools? Try to pour a cold glass of water when you are in the desert with nothing but sand and sun! Making something out of nothing is just not scientifically possible! With exception of creationism, all of the widely accepted theories and hypotheses begin their stories at a point after which *something* already existed! Modern science cannot explain the dilemma of a nothing origin! In fact, there are three basic puzzles that elude scientists: time, matter, and space. There are many questions and unknowns about the content and rules surrounding these three puzzles. For example, what are the boundaries of space and what exists on the other side of those boundary lines? However, the largest unknown to these puzzles is with regard to their origin. Scientists have not been, nor will they ever be, able to explain the origin of time, matter, or space as long as they continue searching for an explanation that ignores intelligent design. I would like to take a moment to clarify that some scientists promote intelligent design, but the louder voice coming from the scientific community is that of opposition. Belief in intelligent design is a perspective that views our environment as too complex to be accidental; therefore, it must have been designed by an intelligent agent.

Since science is powerless to explain the origin of the atom, element, or matter, there is only one logical explanation in existence today, which is creation. There are multiple creation stories from various cultures, but we will focus on the Biblical story of creation in this book. The Bible has undergone scrutiny for thousands of years, but no one has ever found a legitimate inconsistency or error! Only intelligent creation explains how particles, that did not previously exist, were generated from nothing and came together to form something.

The big bang theory attempts to explain how worlds and living creatures were initialized, but it fails to explain how the particles that exploded were first formed. Where did the exploding particles come from? If nothing existed then there was nothing to explode! What was the origin of the gases that burn perpetually in order to provide light and heat to the earth? How did all of these *somethings* in our universe come from a blank slate of nothing? The truth is that God spoke particles of matter into existence. As He spoke, worlds and stars began to form; each took their position in the heavens as if they were being arranged in a cabinet. Massive collections of rock and dirt clung together in perfect sequence like a symphony guided by a maestro's baton.

> In the beginning God created the heaven and the earth. And the earth was without form, and void; and darkness was upon the face of the deep. And the Spirit of God moved upon the face of the waters. And God said, Let there be light: and there was light. And God saw the light, that it was good: and God divided the light from the

darkness. And God called the light Day, and the darkness he called Night. And the evening and the morning were the first day. (Genesis 1:1-5, KJV)

And God said, Let there be lights in the firmament of the heaven to divide the day from the night; and let them be for signs, and for seasons, and for days, and years: And let them be for lights in the firmament of the heaven to give light upon the earth: and it was so. And God made two great lights; the greater light to rule the day, and the lesser light to rule the night: he made the stars also. And God set them in the firmament of the heaven to give light upon the earth, And to rule over the day and over the night, and to divide the light from the darkness: and God saw that it was good. And the evening and the morning were the fourth day. (Genesis 1:14-19, KJV)

During a message several years ago, Reverend Joe McKnight commented that all of creation exists inside of God. God does not exist around every corner and between every nook of creation; instead, He is actually the medium in which everything else is created. As the medium of creation, God does not only surround, but also exists through everything in the entirety of our universe! God is similar to the frame of a painting over which the earth and heavens are stretched; the planets are suspended upon Him. Moses tells us that God spoke our universe into existence (Genesis 1:1-19, KJV). Matter is not a derivative of God's Spirit; it has an origin, but God's Spirit has always existed. Before creation there was neither matter nor any miniature or primitive particles. At that point, there was literally nothing, but on the first day of creation there was something! Days, weeks, and years did not exist until God created them. At the command of God, time, matter, and space sprang into existence. Accident and happenstance are woefully inadequate when attempting to explain what happened on day one of our universe! Emptiness can only be filled through intentional means, and intent is only half of the story. The other half of the story is ability. Day one could only be accomplished through intentional design by an Almighty God!

Defining God

We previously discussed how God's creation consists of time, space, and matter. In the late 1700's, a man by the name of Antoine Lavoisier is credited with developing the theory of

Conservation of Mass, which states that matter can neither be created nor destroyed (Donovan, 2020). Albert Einstein later built upon this concept with his theory of Special Relativity, which asserts that mass and energy are interchangeable; in special circumstances each can be converted to the other (The Editors of Encyclopedia Britannica, 2018). Matter cannot be destroyed; it can only be converted to energy. This concept is perfectly logical because humans are powerless to destroy what God brought into existence. When was the last time you saw someone destroy space? Have humans ever obliterated or manipulated time? God is the Creator as well as the keeper of His creation. Why does God exist in all four corners of His creation? It is because all creation exists inside of Him; He is the inventor, the structure, and the keeper of His creation.

> One God and Father of all, who is above all, and through all, and in you all. (Ephesians 4:6, NKJV)

> The eyes of the Lord are in every place, beholding the evil and the good. (Proverbs 15:3, KJV)

> Can any hide himself in secret places that I shall not see him? saith the Lord. Do not I

fill heaven and earth? saith the Lord.
(Jeremiah 23:24, KJV)

Whither shall I go from thy spirit? or
whither shall I flee from thy presence? If I
ascend up into heaven, thou art there: if I
make my bed in hell, behold, thou art
there. If I take the wings of the morning,
and dwell in the uttermost parts of the sea;
Even there shall thy hand lead me, and thy
right hand shall hold me. (Psalm 139:7-10,
KJV)

If God is larger than His creation and all creation exists inside of Him, what are the characteristics of God? Paul explained the size of God: He is above, surrounding, and inside of everything (Ephesians 4:6, NKJV). This characteristic of God is known as omnipresence. God literally exits in every place all at once. According to Solomon, God can see everything that happens in every place (Proverbs 15:3, KJV). Jeremiah documented, "Do not I fill heaven and earth? saith the Lord" (Jeremiah 23:24, KJV). David said, "Where can I go from Your Spirit?" (Psalm 139:7, KJV). There is no place on earth, in earth, or in the universe where we can escape God! He resides at your starting point, everywhere during your journey, and is waiting on you at your destination. He is literally everywhere!

> No one has seen God at any time. The only begotten Son, who is in the bosom of the Father, He has declared Him. (John 1:18, NKJV)

> For God is not the author of confusion but of peace, as in all the churches of the saints. (1 Corinthians 14:33, NKJV)

John tells us that God is invisible and has never been seen (John 1:18, NKJV). This is logical since God is a spirit, and spirits cannot be seen by the human eye. A God that exists everywhere has to be invisible and consist of something other than matter, otherwise He would defy physics. In physics, the Pauli Exclusion Principle is applicable to many forms of matter; it states, "No two electrons in an atom can be at the same time in the same state or configuration" (The Editors of Encyclopedia Britannica, 2018). If God consisted of matter then He would not be able to exist in the same physical space as a rock or a tree. However, remember that God designed and created time, matter, and space, which means He also created the laws of physics.

Mankind only observed and named these laws many years after God created them! However, God is not constructed of atoms; therefore, His Spirit can occupy the same space as matter without violating His physical laws! God created and designed all things according to His own order; He would not violate His own law because He does not author confusion. Additionally, even if God were visible it would still be impossible for humans to see Him because of the scale differential between mankind and God. Humans are miniscule in comparison to a God that is larger than the universe. Imagine a dust mite being able to see and recognize a dog while buried in the dog's fur. Our physical limitations simply do not allow us to see God even though He is so close that He is touching our skin! Our inability to see God is not evidence of God's absence; it is simply evidence of our limitations!

> O lord, thou hast searched me, and known me. Thou knowest my downsitting and mine uprising, thou understandest my thought afar off. Thou compassest my path and my lying down, and art acquainted with all my ways. For there is not a word in my tongue, but, lo, O Lord, thou knowest it altogether. (Psalm 139:1-4, KJV)

> Remember the former things of old, For I
> am God, and there is no other; I am God,
> and there is none like Me, Declaring the
> end from the beginning, And from ancient
> times things that are not yet done, Saying,
> My counsel shall stand, And I will do all My
> pleasure. (Isaiah 46:9-10, NKJV)

We know that God is omnipresent and invisible, but what else does the Bible say about God? David informs us that God knows our very thoughts (Psalm 139:1-4, KJV). Isaiah tells us that God knows what will transpire before it happens (Isaiah 46:10, NKJV). These verses explain how God's knowledge consists of everything. He can recall anything that has happened just as He can predict anything that will happen! The mind of God is omniscient! Nothing is hidden, nor can anything hide, from God! He knows the end from the beginning; our past and our future!

> Have you not known? Have you not heard?
> The everlasting God, the Lord, The Creator
> of the ends of the earth, Neither faints nor
> is weary. His understanding is
> unsearchable. (Isaiah 40:28, NKJV)

> As for the Almighty, we cannot find Him;
> He is excellent in power, In judgment and
> abundant justice; He does not oppress.
> (Job 37:23, NKJV)

Isaiah informs us that God is everlasting, the Creator of all things, and does not grow weary (Isaiah 40:28, NKJV). God's power is unrivaled and limitless; He is omnipotent! God does not have to eat, sleep, or exercise in order to maintain His energy levels. He does not tire after a long day of strenuous work or a sleepless night; in fact, God does not sleep or rest at all! His power has no cap or limit, it is immeasurable; His abilities are innumerable! Earlier we mentioned building a car without tools or raw materials. God's power is so great that He started with nothing and created everything we see, hear, feel, smell, and taste! There is no power that rivals God's power because everything was created by Him. We have only the power that He allows us to have. Our abilities and intelligence were designed and developed by Him!

> For I am the Lord, I do not change;
> Therefore you are not consumed, O sons of
> Jacob. (Malachi 3:6, NKJV)

> In hope of eternal life, which God, that
> cannot lie, promised before the world
> began. (Titus 1:2, KJV)

Malachi tells us that God is immutable; He never changes (Malachi 3:6, NKJV). God had all of His characteristics before creation, and He will retain all of His characteristics throughout eternity! He always was and will always be! Not only will God remain the same, but Paul informs us that God cannot lie (Titus 1:2, KJV). When God says something it happens! God is the most consistent and dependable entity that will ever exist! Nothing that happens during our lifetime, the lifetime of anyone before us, or the lifetime of anyone after us will change God's characteristics! His longevity is without end!

God is invisible, infinite, immutable, omniscient, omnipotent, omnipresent, and eternal! God is invisible; therefore, His Spirit has never and will never be seen. God is infinite because He cannot be measured. God is immutable because He will never change! God is omniscient because He knows everything that has happened or will ever happen. God is omnipotent because He holds all power in heaven and earth. God is omnipresent because He exists everywhere at all times. God is eternal because He has no beginning nor will He have an end! The characteristics of God should act as the prism through which we view Him, and it should be the benchmark against which we compare everything else we know or learn about God! It can be easy to lose sight of God's attributes when we examine His interaction with humans and how He acts towards us!

God's everywhere existence, or omnipresence, differs greatly from His manifest presence. A manifestation is simply when an invisible substance begins to display, appear, or physically represent itself in a manner that can be detected by one of the five human senses. If we cannot see, smell, taste, feel, or hear something, we are typically unaware of its presence. Manifest means to take something, which cannot be detected, and display it in such a way as to make it obvious or render it detectible. You may be familiar with this word as it relates to medical health conditions. For instance, cancer is unlikely to be diagnosed unless a patient manifests signs, such as tumors or failure in bodily function. It is the physical manifestation that typically brings awareness of the illness. In this analogy, a tumor is considered a manifestation of the cancer. When we look through the Bible, we see that many people did not recognize the presence of God until He manifested Himself through some physical manner. One of the fundamental characteristics of God is that He exists everywhere all of the time; however, God also chooses to manifest Himself in ways that get our attention!

The limitless nature of God is a critical concept that we must grasp in order to fully understand God, and avoid becoming confused by the actions of God. Looking at the details of how God moved or acted throughout history can cause some people to become lost in the minutia of His action, and lose sight of the big picture of His Spiritual characteristics. We often become like the dust mite stuck in the dog fur! The way God acts should never be confused with the attributes of God Himself! God is and will always be larger and more powerful than His creation. As a result of His power, He can manifest Himself to His creation in any way He prefers. Multiple manifestations of God do not equal multiple gods; it only means that He is relating to us on a lower, simplified level due to our physical limitations. We cannot truly fathom a God that exists outside of creation because our knowledge and imagination ends at the boundaries of creation. However, we can trust and believe the Word of God when He tells us about His characteristics!

Physical Acts of a Spiritual God

> And the Lord went before them by day in a
> pillar of a cloud, to lead them the way; and

by night in a pillar of fire, to give them light; to go by day and night. (Exodus 13:21, KJV)

As he journeyed he came near Damascus, and suddenly a light shone around him from heaven. Then he fell to the ground, and heard a voice saying to him, Saul, Saul, why are you persecuting Me? (Acts 9:3-5, NKJV)

And the angel of the Lord appeared unto him in a flame of fire out of the midst of a bush: and he looked, and, behold, the bush burned with fire, and the bush was not consumed. And Moses said, I will now turn aside, and see this great sight, why the bush is not burnt. And when the Lord saw that he turned aside to see, God called unto him out of the midst of the bush, and said, Moses, Moses. And he said, Here am I. (Exodus 3:2-4, KJV)

And mount Sinai was altogether on a smoke, because the Lord descended upon it in fire: and the smoke thereof ascended as the smoke of a furnace, and the whole mount quaked greatly. (Exodus 19:18, KJV)

And the Lord appeared unto him in the plains of Mamre: and he sat in the tent door in the heat of the day; And he lift up his eyes and looked, and, lo, three men stood by him: and when he saw them, he ran to meet them from the tent door, and bowed himself toward the ground. (Genesis 18:1-2, KJV)

Then they brought the gold vessels that had been taken from the temple of the house of God which had been in Jerusalem; and the king and his lords, his wives, and his concubines drank from them. They drank wine, and praised the gods of gold and silver, bronze and iron, wood and stone. In the same hour the fingers of a man's hand appeared and wrote opposite the lampstand on the plaster of the wall of the king's palace; and the king saw the part of the hand that wrote. (Daniel 5:3-5, NKJV)

Even though God is an invisible spirit, several times throughout history He chose to manifest Himself to His creation in physical, earthly forms. Moses helps us see that God displayed Himself to the Israelites as a cloud and fire (Exodus 13:21, KJV). God was exactly what the Israelites needed at the moment they needed Him! They needed protection from the Egyptians, direction to the Promised Land, spiritual guidance, and emotional support throughout their journey! Luke documented that God manifested Himself to Paul in the form of a blinding light (Acts 9:3, NKJV). Paul was so blinded by his religion that it took a blinding light to get his attention and help him see God! Paul was traveling to capture and harass Christians when God shined a light in his eyes that caused blindness for three days! This was the turning point in Paul's life. From this point, he began to follow after Christ instead of persecute Him! God manifested Himself to Moses as a fire and voice coming from a burning bush (Exodus 3:2-4, KJV). Moses was hiding in the desert from his past, but he was unable to hide from God! God changed the course of Moses' life and set him on a journey of obedience. Moses became so close to God that they would speak face to face as friends! God also manifested Himself to Moses and the Israelites on Mount Sinai in the form of fire and smoke (Exodus 19:18, KJV). On another occasion, Moses recorded that God manifested

Himself to Abraham in the form of a man (Genesis 18:1-2, KJV). Daniel wrote of an instance where God appeared at a party hosted by the king of Babylon in order to inform the king of his impending defeat to the Medes and Persians (Daniel 5:5, NKJV). This verse tells us that God manifested Himself to Belshazzar as a partial hand of a man that wrote a message on the wall.

There are many other examples, but we will not list them all here. Suffice to say that God uses physical manifestations in order to accomplish His goals, and visual representations in order to gain our undivided attention! When God manifests Himself in a visible, tangible form it is in order to fulfill a specific purpose. We discussed that God captured Paul's attention in the form of light, gave a sign to the Israelites in the form of smoke, and delivered a message concerning His plans for Sodom and Gomorrah when He visited Abraham as a human. Using this precedent, God chose a manifestation as the catalyst to deliver a message of hope and deliverance to His creation! He chose to manifest Himself in the body of a man, and suffer affliction and death in order to become the savior of the world!

> And without controversy great is the
> mystery of godliness: God was manifested

in the flesh, Justified in the Spirit, Seen by
angels, Preached among the Gentiles,
Believed on in the world, Received up in
glory. (1 Timothy 3:16, NKJV)

Paul tells us an abbreviated story of Jesus Christ when he
describes the human manifestation of the invisible God (1
Timothy 3:16, NKJV). Paul informs us that God literally created
a human in order to manifest, or make known, His Spirit to all
of us! In this verse, "manifested" comes from the Greek word
that means: to make visibly clear or known (Strong, Phaneroo
Meaning in Bible - New Testament Greek Lexicon - King James
Version 1890). What method did God use to make Himself
visibly clear and known? According to Paul, God became visibly
clear and known by displaying Himself through the human
flesh of Jesus the Christ!

And I will put enmity between thee and the
woman, and between thy seed and her
seed; it shall bruise thy head, and thou
shalt bruise his heel. (Genesis 3:15, KJV)

Brethren, I do not count myself to have
apprehended; but one thing I do,
forgetting those things which are behind

and reaching forward to those things which
are ahead, I press toward the goal for the
prize of the upward call of God in Christ
Jesus. (Philippians 3:13-14, NKJV)

In the Bible, Jesus is referred to many times as the Son of man, but the promise was given to the woman when God said her seed would have ultimate victory over Satan (Genesis 3:15, KJV). The verbiage of this verse was not accidental; instead, it foreshadowed the fact that the Messiah would make His entry to earth by means of a virgin birth. As a result of His ultimate sacrifice, all mankind would have an opportunity to take part in His victory over sin and Satan. At the end, Jesus will defeat Satan once and for all by casting him into the lake of fire, but, in the meantime, we can all celebrate in the victory He obtained over sin when He died on the cross!

This victory offers us salvation because it grants us mercy even though we deserve judgment. The salvation we can obtain is both immediate and sustaining. This salvation is immediate because, as soon as we obey the plan of salvation, we are immediately free from the debt of sin that we accrued up to that moment! It is sustaining because we have the opportunity to be reconciled back to Christ each time sin reenters our life. This is not a free pass to sin, but offers us a path to Christ that is attainable!

It is not only a walk to God, but a walk with God! He continually helps improve our state by leading us closer to Him, and He allows room for error in case we stumble and fall. This continual walk with God is described by Paul as choosing to "press toward the mark" (Philippians 3:14, NKJV). We know that sin causes a gulf between mankind and God; therefore, to avoid this gulf, we must make a decision to abandon things in life that cause us to stumble. Because we are human it is likely that we will stumble; therefore, we continually ask forgiveness, abandon sin, and continue our journey with Christ. With time, we draw closer and closer to God and increasingly look like Him in the process!

> But there shall by no means enter it
> anything that defiles, or causes an
> abomination or a lie, but only those who
> are written in the Lamb's Book of Life.
> (Revelation 21:27, NKJV)

> He who overcomes shall inherit all things,
> and I will be his God and he shall be My
> son. But the cowardly, unbelieving,
> abominable, murderers, sexually immoral,

> sorcerers, idolaters, and all liars shall have
> their part in the lake which burns with fire
> and brimstone, which is the second death.
> (Revelation 21:7-8, NKJV)

> For the wages of sin is death, but the gift of
> God is eternal life in Christ Jesus our Lord.
> (Romans 6:23, NKJV)

John tells us why salvation is necessary (Revelation 21:27, NKJV). In this verse, he informs those that participate in Christ's victory over sin that their names will be written in the Lamb's book of life! This is a requirement to enter into eternity with Christ! Those that overcome with Christ will live with Christ. Adversely, those that do not overcome sin will be separated from Christ for eternity.

We spoke about Satan being cast into the lake of fire; the lake is prepared for him due to his disobedience. When sin is victorious the results are tragic; the reward will go to the victor. If we do not partake in Christ's victory over sin, we will be held responsible for paying the debt that we all accrue through sin. Salvation can now be achieved by anyone willing to take up the cross of Christ and lay down the sin of this world! Anyone and everyone can take full advantage of this glorious opportunity by turning from our wicked ways and following the path that Jesus exemplified. We cannot earn salvation through our own work; however, overcoming sin requires work!

> Then He said to them all, If anyone desires to come after Me, let him deny himself, and take up his cross daily, and follow Me. For whoever desires to save his life will lose it, but whoever loses his life for My sake will save it. (Luke 9:23-24, NKJV)
>
> And the Lord said, Simon, Simon! Indeed, Satan has asked for you, that he may sift you as wheat. (Luke 22:31, NKJV)
>
> For we do not wrestle against flesh and blood, but against principalities, against powers, against the rulers of the darkness of this age, against spiritual hosts of wickedness in the heavenly places. (Ephesians 6:12, NKJV)

Because of Jesus' victorious human sacrifice, He is known throughout the Bible as the Lamb of God. The sacrifice of Jesus became our salvation. Since Christ died on the cross for us, Luke records that we should also take up our cross daily for

Him (Luke 9:23, NKJV). The walk with Christ is daily; I might even say hourly or moment by moment. The enemy of our souls does not limit attacks to once per day or week. Jesus told Peter that Satan desires to have him in order to destroy him. When we desire something, we pursue it, which is exactly what the enemy does to us! Paul says, "We wrestle against...spiritual...wickedness" (Ephesians 6:12, NKJV). It is a continual fight, and, in order to win the war, we must continuously be alert and ready to wage battles against the enemy of our soul!

> Then Moses called for all the elders of Israel, and said unto them, Draw out and take you a lamb according to your families, and kill the passover. And ye shall take a bunch of hyssop, and dip it in the blood that is in the bason, and strike the lintel and the two side posts with the blood that is in the bason; and none of you shall go out at the door of his house until the morning. (Exodus 12:21-22, KJV)

> Now the Lord called to Moses, and spoke to him from the tabernacle of meeting, saying, Speak to the children of Israel, and

say to them: When any one of you brings
an offering to the Lord, you shall bring your
offering of the livestock—of the herd and
of the flock. If his offering is a burnt
sacrifice of the herd, let him offer a male
without blemish; he shall offer it of his own
free will at the door of the tabernacle of
meeting before the Lord. (Leviticus 1:1-3,
NKJV)

The next day John saw Jesus coming
toward him, and said, Behold! The Lamb of
God who takes away the sin of the world!
(John 1:29, NKJV)

God began preparing the Israelites when they were in Egypt.
The only thing that distinguished the Israelites from the
Egyptians was the blood of the lamb. The death of a lamb
signified payment; the people of God were identifiable only by
the lamb's blood. If you read the full story, you will see that the
death angel killed all of the firstborn male children in Egypt,
which included both Egyptian and Israeli households. The angel
bypassed the houses where the lamb's blood was applied to
the door. Notice that the identity did not come from human
ancestry, but from the lamb's blood on the door! Both Egyptian

and Israeli children died except for those with visible identification! This was an early indicator of how God desires to separate His people from those who oppose Him; it is through a process of identity. God desires for His people to cover their sins in His blood and adopt a new lifestyle. This new lifestyle makes us recognizable by appearance, action, attitude, and speech; God values righteousness!

The festival of Passover first began when the Israelites were spared from the death angel (Exodus 12:24-27, KJV). This annual Jewish festival has been observed for thousands of years! We see instances where this festival was observed all throughout the Bible. As part of this festival, a blemish free lamb is killed and eaten (Exodus 12:5-8, KJV). It is not by accident that Jesus Christ was killed on this holiday; He was sacrificed as a spotless Lamb of God (Matthew 26:19; 27:1-37, NKJV). If, in this festival, Jesus is represented by the spotless lamb then we are the Hebrews that sacrificed and ate the lamb. We crucify Jesus each time we are disobedient to God's Word; He had to die because of our sin (Hebrews 6:4-6, KJV). Christ did not die for people that predeceased Him. He died for everyone that was alive at His death and for everyone born thereafter! Continuing with the symbolism of the Passover feast, we eat the lamb when we consume the Word of God, and we make His sacrifice meaningful when we allow His Word to influence our lives (John 6:51, KJV).

At this point in time, the Israelites did not have the Bible to help them understand right from wrong; therefore, shortly after this first Passover, He gave them the Ten Commandments and the Levitical law. God used a man that was already in relationship with Him in order to help draw all of the Israeli people into relationship. We know that He continued to give the Israelites guidance through the prophets; this guidance became our Old Testament. In chapter two of this book, we delve deeper into why God began to cultivate a relationship with the Israeli people; therefore, we will avoid this topic for now.

When God gave Moses the Levitical law, He gave them a process that would allow them to defer judgment for their sins. This process called for a sacrifice that would be offered up to God as atonement for sins. This atonement was only a temporary payment, but offered them reprieve for one year. The process was repeated every year in order to continually defer the due date of full payment. The sacrifice of innocent animals foreshadowed the perfect, sinless sacrifice that Jesus Christ would offer for all of our sins.

John the Baptist knew the Messiah would come to earth as a man, and it appears he had knowledge that the Messiah would give His life in order to permanently atone for the sins of the world because he greeted Jesus as "the Lamb of God" (John 1:29, NKJV). Why else would John publically use this metaphorical title? John was undoubtedly aware of Isaiah's prophecy about the Messiah being led as a lamb to the slaughter, so it is possible that he was simply quoting Isaiah (Isaiah 53:7, NKJV). Jesus was obviously human, but was fulfilling a role that, up to that time, had been reserved for animals. John declared, either knowingly or unwittingly, that Jesus would die as the final sacrifice for the sins of all mankind.

> And He took with Him Peter and the two sons of Zebedee, and He began to be sorrowful and deeply distressed. Then He said to them, My soul is exceedingly sorrowful, even to death. Stay here and watch with Me. He went a little farther and fell on His face, and prayed, saying, O My Father, if it is possible, let this cup pass from Me; nevertheless, not as I will, but as You will. (Matthew 26:37-39, NKJV)

For Jesus to be the Lamb of God, He had to have the characteristics of a Lamb. The limitations God placed on the human body of Jesus were severe. This body originated in the womb of a woman, and it was subject to every mortal limitation. The same limitations that every person throughout history has experienced since sin entered the world through Adam and Eve. The body of Jesus was weak, corruptible, vulnerable to temptation, susceptible to illness, prone to fatigue, and limited in every other human manner. In other words, Jesus was exactly like each and every one of us!

We are able to see Jesus' human weakness when He anguished over giving His own life as a sacrifice for all mankind. "If it is possible", Jesus Christ said, "let this cup pass from Me" (Matthew 26:39, NKJV). At this point, Jesus was well aware of the prophecies of Isaiah as well as others concerning the Messiah; He had also been counseled and trained all of His life by the Holy Spirit. From birth until the prayer in the garden, Jesus had been preparing for the moment when He would sacrifice His life. Jesus knew the purpose for the Messiah was to save all of mankind from their sins; He also knew He was destined to offer His own body as this saving sacrifice. However, Jesus' human flesh did not want to die; He did not want to experience the pain, sorrow, and oppression associated with crucifixion.

We know that Christ dreaded His sacrifice because Matthew recalled, "He [Jesus]...began to be sorrowful and deeply distressed. Then He said to them, 'My soul is exceedingly sorrowful, even to death'" (Matthew 26:37, NKJV). This same verse in the New Living Translation says, "He became anguished and distressed. He told them, 'My soul is crushed with grief to the point of death.'" This is a picture of Jesus under severe dread and apprehension with regard to what was about to happen to Him! If we were faced with Christ's situation, we would likely look for the easiest way out; His humanity wanted to do just that! Thankfully, Jesus did not do as His flesh desired, but He listened to and obeyed the Holy Spirit!

It is difficult to think of Jesus as a man. The mental image we conjure when picturing Him is one where we focus on the miracles He performed, the enchanting events surrounding His birth, and His authority to summon angels from heaven at any moment while He walked on earth. However, the fact still remains that Jesus was born of a woman, which brought with it every humanistic quality. We must somehow bring our minds to fathom the truth that Jesus' natural body had human blood flowing through human veins. His human body required this blood to deliver basic nutrients that were absorbed through His human digestive system, which were ingested in a completely earthly and humanly manner! We have such a reverence for the deity of Jesus, and rightfully so, that we often overlook the human qualities of Jesus. Jesus was and still is a human being!

Recognizing and reverencing His deity is absolutely vital to salvation; however, failing to recognize the physical limitations He placed upon Himself is also detrimental to our spiritual walk. It is detrimental because, without this understanding, we risk falling into the trap of placing the man Christ Jesus on an equal plain as the Spirit of God. God cannot be limited, but the human *man*-ifestation was extremely limited!

Jesus the man is a means by which God chose to manifest Himself to His creation. The body of Jesus is not a separate God from the Spirit of God. We just spoke about an everywhere, or omnipresent, God, and here we are simply focusing in on one of His several manifestations! There is only one God; only one Creator. This one God can choose to utilize an innumerable cache of manifestations that are at His disposal in order to communicate with His creation! Misunderstanding this absolutely critical point is extremely dangerous because elevating Jesus' physical body to that of deity will lend to confusion when reading the Bible, which could cause us to incorrectly perceive conflict concerning the oneness of God!

> Beware lest anyone cheat you through
> philosophy and empty deceit, according to

> the tradition of men, according to the basic
> principles of the world, and not according
> to Christ. For in Him dwells all the fullness
> of the Godhead bodily; and you are
> complete in Him, who is the head of all
> principality and power. (Colossians 2:8-10,
> NKJV)

When Paul penned, "The fullness of the Godhead bodily," he meant all power resides in the physical, transformed body of Jesus Christ (Colossians 2:9, NKJV). All of God's power is concentrated in the body of Jesus. In this way, Jesus is completely human and He is completely God! Paul warns that we should not be fooled by tradition. Tradition might tell us that Christ is one of multiple persons that make up God, but truth tells us that Christ is God in human flesh (Colossians 2:9, NKJV). It is not enough to believe in the Bible; we must know and understand it! If we know the Bible, we will be able to avoid deceit, but, if we are unaware, we will be fooled by tradition. Following Christ requires that we know the Word of God!

The Test

> In that day you will ask in My name, and I
> do not say to you that I shall pray the

Father for you; for the Father Himself loves you, because you have loved Me, and have believed that I came forth from God. I came forth from the Father and have come into the world. Again, I leave the world and go to the Father. (John 16:26-28, NKJV)

Therefore My Father loves Me, because I lay down My life that I may take it again. No one takes it from Me, but I lay it down of Myself. I have power to lay it down, and I have power to take it again. This command I have received from My Father. (John 10:17-18, NKJV)

In order to explain this concept, we will perform a proverbial litmus test by taking the knowledge we learned about Jesus and applying it to a passage of the Bible. Let us look at a verse of the Bible that has the potential to confuse readers, which have not taken Paul's advice to beware of tradition. Humans might use tradition to justify an explanation that Jesus and God are unique entities; in this chapter Jesus almost appears to be speaking as if He is separate from God (John 16:26-28, NKJV). How can Jesus be separate from God if He has the fullness of God residing in His body? The answer is that Jesus, as the Lamb of God, had human thoughts and desires.

Do you remember the limitations of which we spoke earlier? Keep in mind that Jesus is a manifestation of God, so He cannot be a separate god; however, He is one hundred percent human! In the human department, He is no different than you and me! It was imperative for Jesus to have these characteristics because He had to willingly lay down His own life for our sins! There was no external force that commanded Christ to lay down His life; the human Jesus forwent His own human desire and submitted Himself to the will of God.

> Let no one say when he is tempted, I am tempted by God; for God cannot be tempted by evil, nor does He Himself tempt anyone. But each one is tempted when he is drawn away by his own desires and enticed. (James 1:13-14, NKJV)

> Seeing then that we have a great High Priest who has passed through the heavens, Jesus the Son of God, let us hold fast our confession. For we do not have a High Priest who cannot sympathize with our weaknesses, but was in all points

tempted as we are, yet without sin.
(Hebrews 4:14-15, NKJV)

For the flesh lusts against the Spirit, and
the Spirit against the flesh; and these are
contrary to one another, so that you do
not do the things that you wish. (Galatians
5:17, NKJV)

James tells us that God cannot be tempted to sin, but we
know that Jesus Christ was tempted (James 1:13; Hebrews
4:14-15, NKJV). If the full authority and power of God dwells in
the body of Jesus then how can Christ be tempted to sin? Jesus
was completely human, which gave Him all of our weaknesses
and limitations. He needed to be tempted and have free will in
order to willingly choose to obey and submit to the leading of
the Spirit of God. Why is this important? If Jesus was never
tempted then His sacrifice would have been meaningless! The
concept of Jesus forgoing His human will for the will of God
seems foreign to us, but, in fact, it happens every day within
each and every one of us.

The Need

Every human alive today has a spirit and a fleshly body. Our
flesh is constantly warring against our spirit, and, in our fallen

state, most humans allow flesh to overpower their spirit. Before sin entered the world, the spirit was in control and mankind lived in innocence; the flesh was continually subject to the spirit. However, after sin entered the world, mankind was banished from the Garden of Eden, and every human from that time forward was born with a propensity, or a desire, to sin. This is how Jesus was born, and this is what He overcame in order to be the first and only human to ever live a life free from sin! Through temptation, Jesus' sacrifice was made meaningful and provides hope to all mankind! Hope is available only because Jesus overcame, which empowers each of us to overcome!

> Unto the woman he said, I will greatly multiply thy sorrow and thy conception; in sorrow thou shalt bring forth children; and thy desire shall be to thy husband, and he shall rule over thee. And unto Adam he said, Because thou hast hearkened unto the voice of thy wife, and hast eaten of the tree, of which I commanded thee, saying, Thou shalt not eat of it: cursed is the ground for thy sake; in sorrow shalt thou eat of it all the days of thy life; Thorns also and thistles shall it bring forth to thee; and

thou shalt eat the herb of the field; In the
sweat of thy face shalt thou eat bread, till
thou return unto the ground; for out of it
wast thou taken: for dust thou art, and
unto dust shalt thou return. (Genesis 3:16-
19, KJV)

Behold, I was brought forth in iniquity, And
in sin my mother conceived me. (Psalm
51:5, NKJV)

After banishment from the Garden, mankind was no longer
allowed to eat from the tree of life, but, instead, was forced to
eat from a cursed ground. This cursed ground only sustained
the flesh, and mankind was born into sin generation after
generation. This perpetual sin condition brings with it a
countdown that begins once a baby enters into this world. It is
not a matter of whether or not a child will sin during his or her
lifetime, but the only question is this: At what point in his or
her life will each child sin? Desire to sin is part of our fallen
human nature; an intrinsic foe whose victory or defeat will
decide our destiny. Jesus Christ experienced this same fallen
nature, but He overcame it in order to provide an example for
every human born with this condition!

> For all have sinned and fall short of the
> glory of God. (Romans 3:23, NKJV)

> For I know that in me (that is, in my flesh)
> nothing good dwells; for to will is present
> with me, but how to perform what is good
> I do not find. For the good that I will to do,
> I do not do; but the evil I will not to do,
> that I practice. (Romans 7:18-19, NKJV)

What is righteousness? In the most simplified form, righteousness is consistently doing that which is right in the eyes of God. It is our flesh that tempts us to act in a manner that opposes God's plan, design, and desire. People often ask: Is it enough to be a good person? Well the answer is yes! However, what constitutes a good person? A person is only good if he or she meets God's definition, which is perfection without any failure. Today mankind primarily chooses to give in to temptation instead of abstaining from it and ends up missing God's definition of good. Paul said that he wanted to be a good person, but ended up performing evil acts. He said there was nothing good about his flesh!

In order to overpower the evil flesh, we require help from the Holy Spirit! When we allow the Holy Spirit to lead and guide us into all righteousness, we put our flesh under subjection to His Spirit! This is the same Holy Spirit to which Jesus prayed and submitted! This brings us back to the reason Jesus had fleshly desires and temptations; it was all for our benefit! Since our flesh is so weak, we need significant help in order to succeed! He gave us His life as a perfect sinless example in order for us to imitate, and He paid the price for the instances where we fail to follow His example! All we have to do is obey! Jesus has put a process into place where we can try, fail, and try again; His process allows us to repeat this again and again until we finally succeed! The only thing He asks of us is to obey! Whether we obey on our first or one millionth attempt, it is only critical that we ultimately find obedience! The most important thing we can ever do is to exit this life while practicing obedience!

> I say then: Walk in the Spirit, and you shall not fulfill the lust of the flesh. For the flesh lusts against the Spirit, and the Spirit against the flesh; and these are contrary to one another, so that you do not do the things that you wish. But if you are led by the Spirit, you are not under the law. (Galatians 5:16-18, NKJV)

When we read John chapter 16 once again knowing that Jesus was completely human when He walked on earth, it takes on a brand new meaning! We should read with the understanding that a human is explaining to other humans how the Holy Spirit inside of Him is different from His human body. It took faith, courage, and boldness for Jesus, as a human, to believe and convey to others that He is the Messiah! This concept of a Holy Spirit residing inside of an earthly body would be incredibly difficult to explain!

Can you imagine trying to explain this brand new concept for the very first time? At that time, people were required by law to travel to Jerusalem to worship God; however, a man is telling them that He is God in flesh. This would be a hard concept to hear and a difficult message to preach! Jesus Christ was flesh, blood, bone, cartilage, and consisted completely of earthly matter; however, He was also full of the Spirit of Almighty God! Jesus allowed the Holy Spirit to lead and guide Him into victory! Paul instructed us that Jesus still exists today as a human, and all of the power and authority of God is localized within His body (Colossians 2:8-10, NKJV). This enables Jesus to be both a human sacrifice for sin as well as a physical manifestation of the omnipresent God!

TWO

Hear, O Israel

The Abrahamic Covenant

Before we can truly understand the humanity of Jesus, we must first understand the deity of His Spirit. Christianity did not rise from a vacuum; instead, it originated from the Old Testament religion practiced by the Israelites, which is known today as Judaism. According to the Bible's Old Testament, Judaism is a monotheistic religion that dates back approximately four thousand years to a man by the name of Abraham. The religion of Judaism began when God established a covenant, or agreement, with this ancient Hebrew man.

> And when Abram was ninety years old and
> nine, the Lord appeared to Abram, and said
> unto him, I am the Almighty God; walk
> before me, and be thou perfect. And I will

make my covenant between me and thee, and will multiply thee exceedingly. And Abram fell on his face: and God talked with him, saying, As for me, behold, my covenant is with thee, and thou shalt be a father of many nations. Neither shall thy name any more be called Abram, but thy name shall be Abraham; for a father of many nations have I made thee. And I will make thee exceeding fruitful, and I will make nations of thee, and kings shall come out of thee. (Genesis 17:1-6, KJV)

This is my covenant, which ye shall keep, between me and you and thy seed after thee; Every man child among you shall be circumcised. And ye shall circumcise the flesh of your foreskin; and it shall be a token of the covenant betwixt me and you. (Genesis 17:10-11, KJV)

But when you are invited, go and sit down in the lowest place, so that when he who invited you comes he may say to you, Friend, go up higher. Then you will have glory in the presence of those who sit at the table with you. (Luke 14:10, NKJV)

By faith Abraham obeyed when he was called to go out to the place which he would receive as an inheritance. And he went out, not knowing where he was going. (Hebrews 11:8, NKJV)

Almighty God promised Abraham that, if he would "walk before" Him and be "blameless", he would receive a large area of land (Genesis 17:1-6, KJV). The Christian Standard Bible (CSB) translates this as, "I am God Almighty. Live in my presence and be blameless." This should be viewed as an invitation from God to leave his current reality and *go up higher*. Jesus told a parable to a group of lawyers and religious men, which taught of the benefits of humility (Luke 14:7-11, NKJV). In this story, Jesus speaks of a man receiving an invitation to attend a wedding feast. He tells that the man should sit at the least desirable table, and, if he does, he might be called to come closer to the wedding party. Jesus teaches that, through humility, the man may receive honor instead of shame. Applying this paradox to Abraham's story, we see that Abraham is offered a monumental invitation; God invites Abraham to partake in a life of humility in order to come up higher! God promised that if Abraham trusted in God and left behind his old life, he will be rewarded with a life in the presence of the Bridegroom. Abraham was invited to forgo his own will, desires, and ambitions in exchange for selflessness, submission to God, and an obedient lifestyle. God promised that Abraham's life of humility and subordination would enable him to receive honor and glory. God promised to make him the father of many nations and that kings would come from his lineage. Because Abraham was obedient, his name was given notoriety and fame; religions, kings, nations, and multitudes of people have come from his bloodline! Because of Abraham's obedience, he is listed in the Bible's faith hall of fame; Abraham received the call from God and obeyed (Hebrews 11:8, NKJV). This obedience enabled Abraham to inherit his land of promise!

Notice the agreement required Abraham to do something in exchange for the land. This exchange is where the land of Canaan, which is the approximate location of the current nation of Israel, came to be known as the *Promised Land*. The requirement for Abraham was to develop a relationship with God, and, as a result, God deeded the land of Canaan to him and his descendants. Building a relationship with God does not vary greatly from the manner in which humans build relationships with one another. We form emotional bonds through frequent communication and close proximity. We maintain emotional bonds through acts of service, exchanging gifts, spending quality time, verbalizing affection, and physical embrace or touch (Chapman, 2015). A relationship with God is very similar because humans are created to be like Him, this is because God created humans for companionship. This is exemplified by the relationship between God and Adam at the beginning of creation; God developed a close friendship with Adam. The Bible records that He would walk with Adam in the Garden of Eden; God enjoyed spending time with His creation and engaging in conversation with him. Once Adam sinned, it caused a gap that separated him from God. Can you imagine how God was heartbroken by Adam's betrayal? All throughout history, God has worked to close the gap introduced by Adam, and He continues this quest to this very day! Though God desires a relationship with mankind, He will not force us into relationship with Him. He beckons us to come back to Him, but leaves the decision to each of us. Through this exchange with Abraham, we can see how God works to woo mankind back into relationship.

God offered Abraham a land of promise in exchange for his love and emotion. This relationship was passed from Abraham to his son Isaac, from Isaac to his son Jacob, and so forth. The covenant was perpetual from generation to generation; it was not only given to Abraham, but extended to all of his heirs. The Jews, throughout history, would signify their ratification of this covenant with God by circumcising their male children. Any uncircumcised Jewish male was and still is considered by the Jewish community to be outside of the covenant with Almighty God. Over time, the Almighty God, that initiated this covenant, came to be known by the Jewish people as *Yahweh*. God moved men in ancient Israel to write as He spoke through them. These writings were eventually consolidated into one compilation known as the Tanakh; this Jewish Bible consists of the same books as the Old Testament in the Christian Bible (Sarna & Faherty, 2018). In order to preserve these words from God, the Jews would write and rewrite these holy manuscripts over and over. This would ensure that long after the original document had decayed, the word of God would continue to be available. However, as the Jews recorded God's word, they used a system of writing that excluded vowels; every word was written in consonants. Because of this writing technique, no one is certain how to pronounce the name they recorded as: YHWH. However, today it is broadly recognized and written as: Yahweh. Since Christianity was derived from Judaism, it is important to realize that Yahweh, the God of the Jews, is actually the very same God of the Christians. There was no godly transition of absolute power between the Old and New

Testaments of the Bible! A period of approximately four hundred years spanned between the last writings of the Old Testament and the first writings of the New Testament; however, Almighty God did not change during this period of time!

If the Almighty God of Judaism is the same Almighty God of Christianity, why are these two religions separate? Both religions recognize and honor the same deity, so what makes them distinct? The only real distinction between Judaism and Christianity is that people practicing Judaism do not recognize Jesus as the prophesied Messiah, and they do not realize that the covenant has been extended to non-Jew. All throughout the Jewish writings in the Tanakh, a human Messiah is prophesied to come down from heaven and reside here on earth. Since they do not believe Jesus is this prophesied Messiah, they are still waiting for the Messiah's appearance. Also, since they do not recognize Jesus as the Messiah, they do not recognize His nor His disciple's teachings; this means they do not revere the New Testament as God's Word. Regardless, the always present and all-knowing God did not change just because two religions were formed. After all, religion is only a set of rules that govern how mankind treats God. Some religions treat Him very poorly because they do not recognize or revere Almighty God! God is the author of truth; people create religions. Human belief does not change the reality of God!

Heart Circumcision

> For he is not a Jew who is one outwardly, nor is circumcision that which is outward in the flesh; but he is a Jew who is one inwardly; and circumcision is that of the heart, in the Spirit, not in the letter; whose praise is not from men but from God. (Romans 2:28-29, NKJV)

> Therefore remember that you, once Gentiles in the flesh—who are called Uncircumcision by what is called the Circumcision made in the flesh by hands—that at that time you were without Christ, being aliens from the commonwealth of Israel and strangers from the covenants of promise, having no hope and without God in the world. But now in Christ Jesus you who once were far off have been brought near by the blood of Christ. For He Himself is our peace, who has made both one, and has broken down the middle wall of separation, having abolished in His flesh

the enmity, that is, the law of
commandments contained in ordinances,
so as to create in Himself one new man
from the two, thus making peace, and that
He might reconcile them both to God in
one body through the cross, thereby
putting to death the enmity. And He came
and preached peace to you who were afar
off and to those who were near. For
through Him we both have access by one
Spirit to the Father. (Ephesians 2:11-18,
NKJV)

We discussed that the covenant God made with Abraham has been extended to all humanity. Keep in mind this covenant between God and mankind requires circumcision. Paul says that Judaism is no longer established by cutting the skin in circumcision, but now God is recognizing a cutting of the heart! Abraham gave an outward sign to commit to an inward change, but the new covenant is an inward change that leads to outward signs! God now requires a commitment, or covenant, with each and every human that begins to walk before Him as did Abraham. A circumcision of the heart is a change of heart that influences our everyday action. When we enter into covenant with God we become a new person! Our old patterns, habits, and desires are cut away, and we begin to walk in the direction of our God. He is no longer a distant figure, but the relationship has become personal! The New Testament of the Bible tells the story of how the covenant between God and Jew became the covenant between God and all mankind! Gentile was a term Jews used to describe people of non-Hebrew heritage. Paul explained how, at one point in time, Gentiles did not have a relationship with God because they were uncircumcised! Remember that ratification of the covenant required circumcision, which was an unfamiliar practice to the gentiles. This is why gentiles were "strangers from the covenants of promise, having no hope and without God in the world" (Ephesians 2:11-12, NKJV). Paul went on to tell us, "But now in Christ Jesus you...have been brought near by the blood of Christ. For He Himself is our peace, who has made both one, and has broken down the middle wall of separation" (Ephesians 2:13-14, NKJV). Jesus Christ opened the door of relationship to all humanity! Any man or woman who wants relationship with God can circumcise his or her heart and become a participant in the covenant of promise! Paul said, "For through Him we both have access by one Spirit to the Father" (Ephesians 2:18, NKJV).

Instead of welcoming Jesus, the majority of Jews rejected and crucified Him. The Jews not only rejected their Messiah, but also the good news of their Messiah, which is the new covenant of heart circumcision! Because of this rejection, the Jews continue to live under a modified version of the Old Testament, Levitical Law. All humanity has the opportunity to access God; this opportunity can be realized through relationship with God! It is free to anyone who wants it, but it requires circumcision. A heart circumcision is not pleasant; it requires sacrifice. Abraham probably did not want to give up control over his life. Submission is not always easy, but all contracts have stipulations. Contracts offer an exchange; perform the stipulated term and you will receive the benefit of the contract. Entering into covenant with Jesus is no different; it contains both stipulations and benefits! We circumcise our hearts through submission to God's will. God's will includes baptism in water and Spirit; however, we will cover this in greater detail later in this book. If we fulfill our contractual obligations, we will enjoy the everlasting benefits that far outweigh any sacrifice we can offer! Circumcision of the heart is temporarily painful, but a blessed life with Christ will last forever!

The reason Jews did not recognize their Messiah is twofold: 1) they did not understand that their holy scripture prophesies two earthly visits by the Messiah, and 2) they were looking for the signs of His second visitation instead of His first. The Jews were watching and continue to watch for a Messiah that will return in power and might; one that will descend from heaven as a mighty warrior and establish His earthly Kingdom. They were not expecting the humble appearance of Jesus; therefore, they rejected and crucified Him. However, just like His dual appearance on earth, their rejection of Christ had already been foretold in the Bible.

> For He shall grow up before Him as a tender plant, And as a root out of dry ground. He has no form or comeliness; And when we see Him, There is no beauty that we should desire Him. He is despised and rejected by men, A Man of sorrows and acquainted with grief. And we hid, as it were, our faces from Him; He was despised, and we did not esteem Him. Surely He has borne our griefs And carried our sorrows; Yet we esteemed Him stricken, Smitten by God, and afflicted. But He was wounded for our transgressions, He was bruised for our iniquities; The chastisement for our peace was upon Him, And by His stripes we are healed. All we like sheep have gone astray; We have

turned, every one, to his own way; And the
Lord has laid on Him the iniquity of us all.
He was oppressed and He was afflicted, Yet
He opened not His mouth; He was led as a
lamb to the slaughter, And as a sheep
before its shearers is silent, So He opened
not His mouth. (Isaiah 53:2-7, NKJV)

And one will say to him, What are these
wounds between your arms? Then he will
answer, Those with which I was wounded
in the house of my friends. (Zechariah 13:6,
NKJV)

And in that day His feet will stand on the
Mount of Olives, Which faces Jerusalem on
the east. And the Mount of Olives shall be
split in two, From east to west, Making a
very large valley; Half of the mountain shall
move toward the north And half of it
toward the south. (Zechariah 14:4, NKJV)

The Holy text of the Jews proclaims that their Messiah
would be despised, rejected, chastised, oppressed, wounded,
and afflicted. All of these verbs are descriptive of how Jesus
was treated! Isaiah prophesied, "Yet He opened not His

mouth" (Isaiah 53:7, NKJV). Jesus took criticism, abuse, and torture, but remained silent. During His first appearance on earth, He was led by the Holy Spirit and fulfilled many of the Old Testament prophecies concerning the Messiah! Instead of recognizing Jesus through fulfilled Old Testament prophecy, the Jews chose disbelief and now they continue to wait for Him. One day their wait will be over when Jesus returns to earth a second time! When Jesus returns, the Jews will recognize Him because He will fulfill the prophecies of Zechariah. The feet of Jesus will touch down on the Mount of Olives in Jerusalem, and the Jews will know that their Messiah has finally arrived! They will notice the scars in His hands and ask Him: Where did you obtain these wounds? According to Zechariah, Jesus' reply will be, "I was wounded in the house of my friends" (Zechariah 13:6, NKJV). Immediately after hearing His response, the Jews will realize their error and recognize their Messiah! His second coming will be much different than His first! He will return as the mighty King for which the Jews currently await. It is unfortunate that the Jews are two thousand years late in recognizing Him! Despite all of the prophetic signs that pointed directly to Jesus, only a small portion of people followed and obeyed His teachings the first time He was here. This will not occur at His second coming!

> Therefore the Lord Himself will give you a
> sign: Behold, the virgin shall conceive and
> bear a Son, and shall call His name
> Immanuel. (Isaiah 7:14, NKJV)

> For unto us a Child is born, Unto us a Son is
> given; And the government will be upon
> His shoulder. And His name will be called
> Wonderful, Counselor, Mighty God,
> Everlasting Father, Prince of Peace. (Isaiah
> 9:6, NKJV)

Approximately two thousand years ago, the Jews lived out the fulfillment of their Holy texts; some of these stories have been preserved for posterity in the Bible's New Testament. The Jews, at that time as well as subsequent generations, have refused to accept or acknowledge the fulfillment of these old prophecies. Just like the Messiah is prophesied to come in power and might, He was also prophesied to be born as a child. How can the Messiah come to earth as both a full grown man and as an infant? How can He descend from heaven causing a catastrophic earthquake as well as be born in a manger and spend many years in weakness and obscurity? How can He return as commander of heavenly armies as well as be abused and remain silent at the hands of His enemies? The Messiah could not possibly enter the world scene and simultaneously fulfill all of these prophecies! This is impossible unless the Old Testament writers were talking about the same man taking part in two separate events!

> Then the angel said to her, Do not be afraid, Mary, for you have found favor with God. And behold, you will conceive in your womb and bring forth a Son, and shall call His name Jesus. He will be great, and will be called the Son of the Highest; and the Lord God will give Him the throne of His father David. And He will reign over the house of Jacob forever, and of His kingdom there will be no end. Then Mary said to the angel, How can this be, since I do not know a man? (Luke 1:30-34, NKJV)

> The woman said to Him, I know that Messiah is coming (who is called Christ). When He comes, He will tell us all things. Jesus said to her, I who speak to you am He. (John 4:25-26, NKJV)

The Messiah was prophesied in the Old Testament book of Isaiah, the birth of the Messiah was recorded in Luke, and

Jesus proclaimed that He is the Messiah in John. The monotheistic God of the Jews in the Old Testament continues unchanged into the New Testament as a monotheistic, all powerful, all knowing, and omnipresent Spirit. The only thing that changed was the birth of the Messiah! The Messiah, which was written about in the Old Testament by Jewish prophets, came to earth as both man and God! A human man who was filled with the Spirit of God! The Messiah came as an earthly, human manifestation of the omnipresent, Almighty God!

> For God so loved the world that He gave His only begotten Son, that whoever believes in Him should not perish but have everlasting life. (John 3:16, NKJV)

> For unto us a Child is born, Unto us a Son is given; And the government will be upon His shoulder. And His name will be called Wonderful, Counselor, Mighty God, Everlasting Father, Prince of Peace. Of the increase of His government and peace There will be no end, Upon the throne of David and over His kingdom, To order it and establish it with judgment and justice From that time forward, even forever. The

zeal of the Lord of hosts will perform this.
(Isaiah 9:6-7, NKJV)

Jesus Christ is the only begotten son of the Father. To be begotten, means to have an origin. Here we see that Jesus has an origin; the Father, or the Spirit of God, does not have an origin. The begotten Son is the son born of Mary; the human Messiah! Judaism is built on the core principle that there is only one all-powerful God, and Jewish prophets prophesied that He would come to earth as a human; therefore, Christians should believe the prophecies and understand that the Messiah is God! Likewise, Christians recognize the Messiah because He fulfilled the prophecies of the Tanakh, or Old Testament; therefore, Jews should also recognize Jesus as Messiah! Isaiah, a Jewish prophet, prophesied that the Messiah would come as a child, be the mighty God, and be the everlasting Father! Isaiah was talking about Jesus; He is the mighty God and the everlasting Father!

> There shall come forth a Rod from the
> stem of Jesse, And a Branch shall grow out
> of his roots. The Spirit of the Lord shall rest
> upon Him, The Spirit of wisdom and
> understanding, The Spirit of counsel and

might, The Spirit of knowledge and of the
fear of the Lord. (Isaiah 11:1-2, NKJV)

And in that day there shall be a Root of
Jesse, Who shall stand as a banner to the
people; For the Gentiles shall seek Him,
And His resting place shall be glorious.
(Isaiah 11:10, NKJV)

And again, Isaiah says: There shall be a root
of Jesse; And He who shall rise to reign
over the Gentiles, In Him the Gentiles shall
hope. (Romans 15:12, NKJV)

To restate what has been discussed, Judaism and
Christianity are not separate religions because the God of
Judaism is also the God of Christianity. Christianity is the
fulfillment of Judaism; the Jews just so happen to be waiting
for a Messiah, as described by Isaiah, which has already been
born and rejected by the Jews approximately two thousand
years ago. Paul told the Christians in Rome that the Messiah
had already come and extended salvation to the Gentiles.
Isaiah also prophesied that salvation would be extended to
non-Israeli people. This aligns perfectly with the topic we
discussed earlier in this chapter concerning the covenant

between God and mankind; the covenant has been extended to non-Jews! The second king of Israel was David, and his father's name was Jesse. Isaiah prophesied that a man of Israeli descent would be born and extend salvation to non-Israeli people. Isaiah informs us, "There shall come forth a Rod from the stem of Jesse...Who shall stand as a banner to the people; For the Gentiles shall seek Him" (Isaiah 11:1; 11:10, NKJV). Paul wrote about this prophecy when he said, "He...shall rise to reign over the Gentiles; in Him the Gentiles shall hope" (Romans 15:12, NKJV). Jesus died for the sins of all mankind and paid the debt for everyone! Our debt is paid if we choose to enter into His covenant!

> In My Father's house are many mansions; if it were not so, I would have told you. I go to prepare a place for you. And if I go and prepare a place for you, I will come again and receive you to Myself; that where I am, there you may be also. (John 14:2-3, NKJV)

We previously discussed God's offer of a land of promise in exchange for Abraham's love and emotion. We just saw where this covenant has been extended to all mankind; however, the land of promise is much greater than a physical plot of dirt!

Jesus said, "I go to prepare a place for you...I will come again...that where I am, there you may be also" (John 14:2-3, NKJV). The covenant still includes a promised land, but it is a much greater promise than what Abraham received. Abraham was only able to inhabit his promised land while He was alive on earth. We will physically reside with God in our land of promise for all eternity! The invitation for Abraham to come up higher has also been extended to all of us! If we are obedient, as Abraham was obedient, we will be able to exchange humility for honor! Instead of having nobility and kings come from our bloodline, we will be grafted into the King's bloodline! Through the new covenant with God, our names will be changed and we will be adopted into the family of God. Our given names will remain the same, but our family, or surname, will be Jesus! We will receive honor because we will be part of an honorable family, the family of God!

To be in the family of God means to have the Spirit of God, which we will discuss later in this book. Earlier in this chapter, we discussed where Isaiah prophesied about Jesus when he said, "The Spirit of the Lord shall rest upon Him, The Spirit of wisdom and understanding, The Spirit of counsel and might, The Spirit of knowledge and of the fear of the Lord" (Isaiah 11:1-2, NKJV). Jesus was continually being counseled by the Holy Spirit from His birth; this is why He had wisdom, understanding, counsel, might, knowledge, and respect for the Lord! Here we see that the spirit of the Lord was prophesied to "rest upon" Jesus, which explains how He knew to avoid sin! Likewise, since the covenant of salvation has been extended to us all, we should seek counsel from the Holy Spirit! We should take advantage of this opportunity to have a relationship with God that counsels us like Jesus was counseled. Many people before us did not have the free access that we enjoy today! We are truly living in the greatest age in all of history!

The Shema

In the beginning God created the heaven and the earth. (Genesis 1:1, KJV)

For a thousand years in thy sight are but as yesterday when it is past, and as a watch in the night. (Psalm 90:4, KJV)

But, beloved, be not ignorant of this one thing, that one day is with the Lord as a thousand years, and a thousand years as one day. (2 Peter 3:8, KJV)

For thus says the High and Lofty One Who inhabits eternity, whose name is Holy: I

dwell in the high and holy place, With him
who has a contrite and humble spirit, To
revive the spirit of the humble, And to
revive the heart of the contrite ones.
(Isaiah 57:15, NKJV)

It is important to keep in mind that God does not change;
He will never change because He is not bound by time. Time is
a concept that began to exist at creation; the Almighty God of
Judaism and Christianity, who is the Creator of all things, is not
subject to His creation. God created time, matter, and space,
and, therefore, existed before their inception. Just as God had
no beginning, He will also have no end; He will exist
forevermore! Time has no influence on God; we see that He
experiences one thousand years the same way He subsists in a
single day! Isaiah says that God inhabits eternity; He has no
beginning and He has no ending! Religions are formed and will
someday vanish away, but the God of the religion is forever!

Hear, O Israel: The Lord our God, the Lord
is one! You shall love the Lord your God
with all your heart, with all your soul, and
with all your strength. And these words
which I command you today shall be in
your heart. You shall teach them diligently

to your children, and shall talk of them when you sit in your house, when you walk by the way, when you lie down, and when you rise up. You shall bind them as a sign on your hand, and they shall be as frontlets between your eyes. You shall write them on the doorposts of your house and on your gates. (Deuteronomy 6:4-9, NKJV)

You are My witnesses, says the Lord, And My servant whom I have chosen, That you may know and believe Me, And understand that I am He. Before Me there was no God formed, Nor shall there be after Me. I, even I, am the Lord, and besides Me there is no savior. (Isaiah 43:10-11, NKJV)

When the Philistines took the ark of God, they brought it into the house of Dagon and set it by Dagon. And when the people of Ashdod arose early in the morning, there was Dagon, fallen on its face to the earth before the ark of the Lord. So they took Dagon and set it in its place again. And when they arose early the next

morning, there was Dagon, fallen on its
face to the ground before the ark of the
Lord. The head of Dagon and both the
palms of its hands were broken off on the
threshold; only Dagon's torso was left of it.
(1 Samuel 5:2-4, NKJV)

God solidified His monotheistic nature in Deuteronomy in
what is commonly referred to as the Hebrew Shema. This truth
is the foundation of the Jewish faith. It is the bedrock on which
all of Judaism is constructed. God instilled within every Jew the
guiding principle that God is one and only One! Moses tells us,
"Hear, O Israel: The Lord our God, the Lord is one"
(Deuteronomy 6:4, NKJV). In this verse, when God tells us to
"Hear" this is intended to get our undivided attention! To what
are we supposed to pay attention? We should understand that
the Lord is one all-powerful God! Isaiah recorded God saying,
"Before Me there was no God formed, Nor shall there be after
Me. I, even I, am the Lord, And besides Me there is no savior"
(Isaiah 43:10-11, NKJV). God is one entity and does not share
power with anyone else; God does not consist of multiple
persons or a multiplicity of anything! God is an ever-present
spirit, which does not allow room for any division! God's spirit
does not have any boundaries or parameters; this is why God

does not consist of a combination or accumulation of tangible persons or beings.

The span of time that transpired between Moses and Isaiah was approximately six hundred and fifty years (Valkanet, 2010). God obviously found it extremely important for His creation to understand His sole supremacy because He reminded the Israelites of this fact again and again for hundreds of years! This message was received by the Jews, and Jews practicing Judaism have this truth memorized from an early age. Jews are taught that any dilution of God is unacceptable and completely false. A God that is in unity with Himself would insinuate that lesser parts are consolidated to form the whole. However, God cannot be described in a numerical value of persons because He is not a person! He cannot be divided, weakened, or fractured in any way! This concept is not complex when we realize that He is simply one all-powerful, ever-present Spirit!

> Thus says the Lord, your Redeemer, And
> He who formed you from the womb: I am
> the Lord, who makes all things, Who
> stretches out the heavens all alone, Who
> spreads abroad the earth by Myself. (Isaiah
> 44:24, NKJV)

Yet I am the Lord your God Ever since the
land of Egypt, And you shall know no God
but Me; For there is no savior besides Me.
(Hosea 13:4, NKJV)

Have we not all one Father? Has not one
God created us? Why do we deal
treacherously with one another By
profaning the covenant of the fathers?
(Malachi 2:10, NKJV)

As we saw earlier, Deuteronomy is not the only book that
plainly exclaims that God is one entity. The references above
are just a few of many where the Old Testament writers
document an unshared, undiluted, sole authority of God.
Isaiah, Hosea, and Malachi make it crystal clear that God does
not share power! Words like I, myself, me, and one are all used
to describe the quantity of God. God's rule is an autocracy, not
an oligarchy. When God makes a decision, He does not have to
convene a meeting in order to draw a consensus; He simply
makes the decision because He has all power! Isaiah recorded
God saying, "I am the Lord...Who stretches out the heavens all
alone" (Isaiah 44:24, NKJV). This does not paint a picture of
division or multiplicity; God does not consist of diverse entities,
He is a single, undivided God with one mind and one will!

Have mercy upon me, O God, According to
Your lovingkindness; According to the
multitude of Your tender mercies, Blot out
my transgressions. Wash me thoroughly
from my iniquity, And cleanse me from my
sin. For I acknowledge my transgressions,
And my sin is always before me. Against
You, You only, have I sinned, And done this
evil in Your sight—That You may be found
just when You speak, And blameless when
You judge. (Psalm 51:1-4, NKJV)

After David committed adultery with Bathsheba and
murdered her husband, we see a distraught and repentant
man pleading with God for forgiveness. In his most dire hour,
David needed to make sure he addressed the right God in
order to obtain forgiveness; he was desperate to remove his
guilt! David said, "Against You, You only, have I sinned, And
done this evil in Your sight" (Psalm 51:4, NKJV). David knew
God and prayed to Him! He did not address multiple entities,
his prayer was simple and directed to the only one that could
forgive him! He went straight to the One God that was
explained to him by his ancestors.

And I prayed to the Lord my God, and
made confession, and said, O Lord, great
and awesome God, who keeps His
covenant and mercy with those who love
Him, and with those who keep His
commandments. (Daniel 9:4, NKJV)

O Lord, hear! O Lord, forgive! O Lord, listen
and act! Do not delay for Your own sake,
my God, for Your city and Your people are
called by Your name. (Daniel 9:19, NKJV)

Daniel prayed on behalf of Israel while in captivity to the
Medes and Persians. His prayer was also directed to one God.
Daniel's reverence, references, and requests were directed to
only one entity he called, "O Lord, great and awesome God"
(Daniel 9:4, NKJV). Daniel said, "O Lord, listen and act...for Your
own sake" (Daniel 9:19, NKJV). Daniel did not call upon a
plethora or counsel of gods, he called upon "the Lord my God"
(Daniel 9:4, NKJV). There was and still is only One that hears
and responds!

And it came to pass, when I heard these
words, that I sat down and wept, and
mourned certain days, and fasted, and
prayed before the God of heaven, And

said, I beseech thee, O Lord God of heaven,
the great and terrible God, that keepeth
covenant and mercy for them that love him
and observe his commandments.
(Nehemiah 1:4-5, KJV)

Nehemiah was serving as cup bearer to the Persian king
Artaxerxes when he received news of how Jews in Jerusalem
were being mistreated and oppressed. Nehemiah was so
distressed by the news that he wept and mourned for them.
He began to fast and pray that God would fulfill His promise to
Moses, which was to restore Israel if they repent of their sins.
Nehemiah did not take the news lightly, he immediately took
action! The action he took was to go to the one source of
power, the God of heaven. Nehemiah prayed, "I beseech thee,
O Lord God of heaven, the great and terrible God, that keepeth
covenant and mercy for them that love him and observe his
commandments" (Nehemiah 1:5, KJV). Yet again we see a man
that is seeking favor from God; the verbiage he uses is clear
and concise. There is not even a hint of respect for any other
deity besides God, and he addresses God directly as one God!

After God told, reminded, and reiterated His Oneness to the
Israelites over and over, we see that they got the point! If you
read the Bible, you will see a story of an on and off relationship

between the Israelites and God; God never stopped loving Israel, but they struggled with maintaining their relationship with Him. You will see that collectively they strayed from God many times throughout history, but, when they needed to get His attention, their prayers to Him are directed towards only one God! They do not address any other God, and they do not recognize or worry about offending any sub-portion of God. They simply call upon the God that is documented all throughout their Tanakh; in this book, He is always a single, all-powerful God! Judaism is unquestionably a monotheistic religion, which means they worship a single God that is not subdivided, split, or segmented in any way!

Since Christianity is a fulfillment of Judaism, monotheism is not just the foundation of Judaism, it is also the foundation of Christianity! Christianity inherits its God from Judaism; therefore, it must also inherit monotheism! If God never changes and He has always been a single entity, it makes sense that He did not divvy Himself up about two thousand years ago. Instead, there is only one God and no one else shares His power! He stands alone as The Almighty, and no other god stands, sits, or kneels beside Him! This was exemplified when the Ark of the Lord was stolen by the Philistines in ancient times; they set the Ark in the temple of their god. Dagon, their handmade god, was knocked over during the night and landed face down before God's Ark of the Covenant. They set him up again, but, on the second night, his head and hands were cut off. God was proving a point that people can wish, hope, believe, or even pray to an entity or figure, but, if the object of our praise is anyone other than the true God, all of our efforts are in vain.

It is hard to imagine a God that stretches forever in the direction of north and forever in the direction of south without ever touching or circling back to His origin. Our minds cannot comprehend a never-ending, no boundaries God! How can anything exist without boundary? Yet to put a boundary on God would defy His nature and quality. He cannot be bound or limited in any way! For this reason, it is impossible for any other deity to exist because any other deity would have to exist inside of God; therefore, any other deity would also consist of God. God is immeasurable, which means He is larger than our imagination; He is unfathomable to our limited brains. There is nowhere you can go to escape God; He is omnipresent. There is no way to fool or trick God; He is omniscient. There is no other deity in the universe besides the one true, living God! He exists everywhere, and nothing was nor ever will be created outside of God. This Supreme Being is God of all power, God of all time, God over all people, and God without boundary. God is absolute, and He is absolutely the God of both Judaism and Christianity!

THREE

God's Face – The Lamb of God

The Promise

We previously discussed how the promise was given to "the woman" (Genesis 3:15, KJV). Even though Eve is the woman that was present when God cursed Satan, the emphasis of the verse is actually placed on Eve's descendant. Mary the mother of Jesus Christ is the subject of this prophecy; Christ is the seed that will ultimately achieve victory over Satan. God promised that the son of woman would have victory over Satan! God was not talking about Cain, Eve's firstborn, nor was He talking about all male children in general. God's promise was immediately preceded by mankind's first sin and was directed towards the one man that would be born into this earth to redeem and restore mankind's relationship with God. He was foreshadowing the earthly visit of the

Messiah; it was a promise that what was lost through sin would someday be restored through salvation!

God is a spirit that cannot be seen by His creation, which makes sense now that we know all of creation is actually inside of God! Since God has the invisible characteristic of a spirit, He devised a mechanism of showing Himself to His creation. God simply followed a pattern that He used many times before. God has utilized manifestations, such as a burning bush and a column of fire, all throughout history. He created a human man in order to accomplish His perfect plan, and, just like many times through various manifestations, He displayed Himself through His creation. Jesus Christ is the interface, or conduit, between God and His creation! He is the point of interaction that enables our access to God!

The Purpose of Mankind

> I am the Lord thy God, which have brought thee out of the land of Egypt, out of the house of bondage. Thou shalt have no other gods before me. Thou shalt not make unto thee any graven image, or any likeness of any thing that is in heaven above, or that is in the earth beneath, or that is in the water under the earth. Thou

shalt not bow down thyself to them, nor serve them: for I the Lord thy God am a jealous God, visiting the iniquity of the fathers upon the children unto the third and fourth generation of them that hate me. (Exodus 20:2-5, KJV)

The first three out of the Ten Commandments, written in stone and delivered to Moses by the hand of God, give us a picture into the nature of God. God tells us, "Thou shalt have no other gods before me" (Exodus 20:3, KJV). God is not admitting that other legitimate gods exist; instead, He is telling us that our time, energy, and affection are precious to Him! If we waste significant portions of our time, energy, or affection on anything that is undeserving, it is the equivalent of serving another god. Anything that takes an unreasonable amount of our attention away from God is taking the place of God in our lives and becomes a false god to us! In today's society, a few common false gods can arise from careers, material possessions, entertainment, and even family! For instance, many parents spend seemingly every moment of available time facilitating or transporting their children between extracurricular school activities, sports practices and games, and entertaining events. Obviously parents love their children and desire to spent time with them; however, this example could be transformed by simply changing the focus of each event to incorporate God!

It is perfectly acceptable to spend time with family, but what are we attempting to accomplish? Do we want our children to be entertained and secularly trained or do we want families that are spiritually equipped and fruitful? Allocating time, energy, and affection for God is critical for every family! Prioritizing family is important, but prioritizing God is paramount. We discussed only one of many scenarios where people deprioritize God for something or someone else. However, the concept to glean from this paragraph is that God, as our Creator and Savior, deserves to be a significant participant in our lives!

> Who exchanged the truth of God for the lie, and worshiped and served the creature rather than the Creator, who is blessed forever. Amen. (Romans 1:25, NKJV)

> Every good gift and every perfect gift is from above, and comes down from the Father of lights, with whom there is no variation or shadow of turning. (James 1:17, NKJV)

For you were bought at a price; therefore
glorify God in your body and in your spirit,
which are God's. (1 Corinthians 6:20, NKJV)

After reading the Ten Commandments, it is easy to see that God cares a great deal about our attention and reverence! In fact, it makes Him angry when people praise and dote upon any false god! Why should it not affect Him? A God that created all things should be recognized as such! The attention and praise of people is so important to God that the very first of His commandments to the Israelites was to recognize Him alone as God. This requirement is not at all unrealistic because God designed, created, and owns all of creation! God tells us that if we praise any part of His creation instead of Him, it will be considered iniquity or sin.

Notice that people cannot treat any person, natural thing, or created object as a god. Also, the second commandment included an order to avoid bowing or serving anyone or anything other than God (Exodus 20:5, KJV). Once again, God is not recognizing the existence of other deities; He is simply cautioning people against treating creation like they should be treating their Creator. Paul discusses this as worship of the creature more than the Creator; he says this is exchanging "the truth of God for the lie" (Romans 1:25, NKJV).

The truth of God is that the Creator, not the creation, should receive all praise! James informs us that, "Every good...and perfect gift is from...the Father" (James 1:17, NKJV). How praise worthy is the recipient of a gift? Not at all, the gift giver should receive the praise! God owns the air we breathe, our physical abilities were designed before we were born, our intellect and power of reason are according to His plan, and the earthly goods in our possession are gleaned from the fruits of His earth. Everything we are and everything we have has been entrusted to us. Paul tells us that our body and our spirit are owned by God (1 Corinthians 6:20, NKJV). For this reason, we are to glorify God with our body and spirit, which means how we present ourselves, our words, our actions, and our affection should all bring glory to God!

Just in case it is not apparent, we were all created for a purpose; no one was accidentally born into this world! God did not forget to turn off His conveyor belt the day you or I rolled off of the assembly line. If you feel that God created you without talent or that your life is meaningless, please know that you were created with intention! If people have misused, battered, or abused you, Jesus still desires your relationship! If you have been cast aside, neglected, or taken for granted, God prioritizes every moment you spend with Him! As long as cognition is present and communication possible, there is a place for you in Christ's Kingdom! We are all extremely valuable to Christ, which is why He died for our sins. His love for us is so strong that He gave His life so that we have the opportunity to retain ours! We should find encouragement in the fact that God has given talent to every person that has ever lived! The feeling of worthlessness and inadequacy does not result from a lack of talent. These feelings are often associated with failing to utilize abilities and skills in the Kingdom of God. If you struggle with finding your purpose, it is this: Use your talent and ability to bring glory to God. If we glorify God in everything we do, our love will be conveyed to Him, and, as a result, we will feel fulfilled in our purpose!

> Then one of them, a lawyer, asked Him a question, testing Him, and saying, Teacher, which is the great commandment in the law? Jesus said to him, You shall love the Lord your God with all your heart, with all your soul, and with all your mind. This is the first and great commandment.
> (Matthew 22:35-38, NKJV)

> Blessed be the Lord God of Israel From everlasting to everlasting! And let all the

people say, Amen! Praise the Lord! (Psalm 106:48, NKJV)

If anyone speaks, let him speak as the oracles of God. If anyone ministers, let him do it as with the ability which God supplies, that in all things God may be glorified through Jesus Christ, to whom belong the glory and the dominion forever and ever. Amen. (1 Peter 4:11, NKJV)

Let this mind be in you which was also in Christ Jesus, who, being in the form of God, did not consider it robbery to be equal with God, but made Himself of no reputation, taking the form of a bondservant, and coming in the likeness of men. And being found in appearance as a man, He humbled Himself and became obedient to the point of death, even the death of the cross. Therefore God also has highly exalted Him and given Him the name which is above every name, that at the name of Jesus every knee should bow, of those in heaven, and of those on earth, and of those under the earth, and that

every tongue should confess that Jesus
Christ is Lord, to the glory of God the
Father. (Philippians 2:5-11, NKJV)

When one of the lawyers asked Jesus about the greatest
commandment, Jesus unequivocally exclaimed that the first of
the Ten Commandments is the greatest! We must love the
Lord God with our heart, soul, and mind! God wants people to
recognize and serve Him alone as God. It is important to
understand how critical praise is to Him! We must reconcile
God's commandments concerning bowing. In the Ten
Commandments, He tells us to avoid bowing to another god,
but He also proclaims in His Word that every knee is going to
bow before Jesus Christ (Philippians 2:10, NKJV). Is there any
conflict or inconsistency with praising, paying homage, or
giving credit to Jesus Christ? If it is a sin to bow to anyone
besides the Almighty God then why is it acceptable to bow to
Jesus Christ? The Psalmist tells us to praise the Lord God of
Israel who is "from everlasting to everlasting" (Psalm 106:48,
NKJV). If God lives forever, it cannot be based on time. For
example, an everlasting God would not desire people's praise
until sometime around A.D. 30 and suddenly cease to care
thereafter; this does not make logical sense! Yet we see Peter
saying Jesus Christ is worthy of praise and dominion forever (1

Peter 4:11, NKJV). Furthermore, Paul tells us that giving praise to Jesus Christ brings glory to God! Praising Jesus Christ is obviously acceptable to God for only one reason: When we praise and bow to Jesus Christ, we are praising and bowing to the Almighty God! Any other scenario would violate God's first and most important commandment!

God Expressing Himself

> God, who at various times and in various ways spoke in time past to the fathers by the prophets, has in these last days spoken to us by His Son, whom He has appointed heir of all things, through whom also He made the worlds; who being the brightness of His glory and the express image of His person, and upholding all things by the word of His power, when He had by Himself purged our sins, sat down at the right hand of the Majesty on high, having become so much better than the angels, as He has by inheritance obtained a more excellent name than they. (Hebrews 1:1-4, NKJV)

Then Mary said to the angel, How can this
be, since I do not know a man? And the
angel answered and said to her, The Holy
Spirit will come upon you, and the power
of the Highest will overshadow you;
therefore, also, that Holy One who is to be
born will be called the Son of God. (Luke
1:34-35, NKJV)

God speaks to His creation through Jesus (Hebrews 1:1-2,
NKJV). Not only does God speak through Jesus, but Jesus is the
"express image of His person" (Hebrews 1:3, NKJV). The
American Standard Version (ASV) Bible translates this passage
as, "The very image of his substance." This verse is not saying
that Jesus resembles or looks like God because that is
impossible; no physical being can look like a spirit. God does
not have any physical features because He is invisible and
exists everywhere. To say God has physical features would limit
God to the boundaries of a face; God is limitless and without
boundary! Instead, this verse is saying that Jesus is a created,
tangible, and visible image of an eternal, invisible, and
intangible God.

We also see that Jesus received His name "by inheritance"
(Hebrews 1:4, NKJV). Jesus, a created being, inherited His name
from God. How does anyone inherit a name? In most modern

societies, one can only inherit something by being a direct descendent; an heir to the family patron or matron. In this instance, Jesus inherited God's name. Mary was shocked to hear that she would become pregnant because she had never been intimate with a man, but the angel explained that her child would be supernaturally created by God in her womb. When we think of inheriting something from our parents, we might think of a physical feature or trait being passed down from generation to generation. However, Jesus did not inherit any physical feature, trait, or characteristic from God because God is not physical in any way; He is only a Spirit. As we just mentioned, Jesus Christ was supernaturally created by God; He is not the offspring of God. This concept is critically important to understand! Jesus was conceived in a virgin girl; therefore, He was formed without male contribution. Christ did not inherit a chromosome from God during the process of becoming the Son of God; the Spirit of God does not have any chromosomes to donate. If Jesus did not inherit any human characteristic from God, what did He inherit? Jesus Christ inherited His very Spirit from God! The phrase "by inheritance" simply means that God's Spirit took up residence in the earthly body of Christ (Hebrews 1:4, NKJV). This Spirit inheritance is how Jesus inherited the name of God (Hebrews 1:4, NKJV).

Inheritance of God's Spirit is accompanied by inheritance of His name!

If Jesus inherited His name from God, that means the name of God must also be Jesus! God speaks through the mouth of Christ, made the worlds through the hands of Christ, expresses Himself through Christ, and even gave His own name to Jesus Christ! We saw earlier that Jesus' name is higher than any other name (Philippians 2:9-10, NKJV). Every knee is going to bow before Jesus, and everyone will exclaim that Jesus is the Lord of heaven and earth! When Jesus is proclaimed as Lord, it will not be similar to a military coup nor will He be overthrowing or superseding God in any way; instead, it will bring glory to God! How can worshipping Jesus Christ bring glory to God? It is because when you and I worship Jesus Christ, we worship Almighty God! When the writer of Hebrews speaks of inheriting the name of Jesus; he is saying the Father's name is Jesus and the Son's name is also Jesus! In other words, both the Spirit of God and the human expression of God have the same name. This is perfectly logical because the Spirit of God is obviously God, and the human Christ is a creation by which God expresses Himself! Jesus is the name of God!

> Look to Me, and be saved, All you ends of
> the earth! For I am God, and there is no

other. I have sworn by Myself; The word has gone out of My mouth in righteousness, And shall not return, That to Me every knee shall bow, Every tongue shall take an oath. He shall say, Surely in the Lord I have righteousness and strength. To Him men shall come, And all shall be ashamed Who are incensed against Him. In the Lord all the descendants of Israel Shall be justified, and shall glory. (Isaiah 45:22-25, NKJV)

And Jesus came and spoke to them, saying, All authority has been given to Me in heaven and on earth. Go therefore and make disciples of all the nations, baptizing them in the name of the Father and of the Son and of the Holy Spirit. (Matthew 28:18-19, NKJV)

We just saw where one day every knee will bow to Jesus, but when this prophecy was originally given by Isaiah, he said every knee will bow to Yahweh, the Almighty God. In fact, God says, "Look to Me...there is no other" (Isaiah 45:22, NKJV). Every human will look unto Jesus and worship Him as God; Jesus Christ is literally the face of God. Jesus is the name of

God, and one day every human will bow their knee before Him admitting that He is The Almighty! Jesus Himself said that He has *all* power in heaven and in earth! He then commanded His disciples to go and baptize in the name of the Father, the name of the Son, and the name of the Holy Spirit. There is not one instance in the Bible where someone was baptized in the titles of Father, Son, and Holy Spirit, but there are several instances where people were baptized in the name of Jesus Christ! This can only mean that the name of God is Jesus, the name of the Son is Jesus, and the name of the Holy Spirit is also Jesus!

> Then Joseph her husband, being a just man, and not wanting to make her a public example, was minded to put her away secretly. But while he thought about these things, behold, an angel of the Lord appeared to him in a dream, saying, Joseph, son of David, do not be afraid to take to you Mary your wife, for that which is conceived in her is of the Holy Spirit. And she will bring forth a Son, and you shall call His name Jesus, for He will save His people from their sins. (Matthew 1:19-21, NKJV)

The Son of Mary inherited the name of God because He is not just the Son of Mary; He is the "express image," or the human body, of God (Hebrews 1:3, NKJV). Jesus inherited His fleshly body from Mary, but inherited God's name when He inherited God's Spirit. We also inherit salvation by receiving God's name; we receive God's name in a similar manner to how Jesus inherited His name. We take on the name of Jesus when the Spirit of God begins to dwell within us! We are made orphans through sin, but we are adopted into the family of God when we are filled with His Holy Spirit! Jesus is the only sacrifice pure enough to wash away our sins; therefore, if we desire eternal life with Him, we absolutely must take advantage of this wonderful opportunity to be part of the family of God!

> Jesus said to him, I am the way, the truth,
> and the life. No one comes to the Father
> except through Me. (John 14:6, NKJV)

Jesus Christ, or God in the resurrected flesh, tells us that He is the only way to God. Why is Jesus the only method to access God? If God loves His people and commands them to worship Him, it would not make sense for God to put a middle-man between Himself and His people! Jesus Christ is the only way to

God because *He is God*. We read earlier that inside of Jesus "dwells all the fullness of the Godhead bodily" (Colossians 2:9, NKJV). How can the head of God dwell in the human body of Jesus? This is Paul's way of saying that God created a body for Himself, and we can worship Jesus Christ as God. We do not have to worry that God will get jealous if we give praise to Jesus or that the Holy Spirit will be green with envy if we spend too much time talking with God. God is still the same as He has always been; He is still only one entity! The only difference is we now have a face and a name to put with our God! His name is Jesus and His face is that of Christ! Christ is the only method of approaching God!

What does it mean for Christ to be the only method of approaching God? Since God is a Spirit, the only way to approach God is through obedience to His Word and through prayer. We will address obedience at a later point, but when we pray to God we should use the name of Jesus. After all, it is the name He donated to Christ! There is only one proper noun to which God responds. In fact, if we pray in titles such as Yahweh, Jehovah, Elohim, Father, Lord, or God, we are not going to invoke the same response from God that is possible by praying in the name of Jesus! Salvation is accomplished, miracles are performed, and prayer is answered through the name of Jesus (Acts 4:8-12, KJV). This passage also tells us that the only way to be saved is through His name! This is the access to God that is accomplished through the name of Jesus!

We learned a moment ago that the human Jesus inherited God's name. God's name was not revealed to creation until the baby was born in Bethlehem about two thousand years ago. Before Jesus was born on earth as a human manifestation of God, God was known to His creation only by titles. The prophet Isaiah foretold that God's name would be revealed through the Messiah; and, at the appropriate time, the name of God was revealed by an Angel to Mary the mother of Jesus. Mary did not name her child; the angel informed Mary of her child's name! Since the angel proclaimed His name to be Jesus, we see that there is significance attached to His name! If the name of Jesus is significant, what does it mean?

> Who, being in the form of God, did not
> consider it robbery to be equal with God,
> but made Himself of no reputation, taking
> the form of a bondservant, and coming in
> the likeness of men. And being found in
> appearance as a man, He humbled Himself
> and became obedient to the point of
> death, even the death of the cross.
> Therefore God also has highly exalted Him
> and given Him the name which is above

every name, that at the name of Jesus
every knee should bow, of those in heaven,
and of those on earth, and of those under
the earth, and that every tongue should
confess that Jesus Christ is Lord, to the
glory of God the Father. (Philippians 2:6-
11, NKJV)

Notice how Paul phrased his explanation of Jesus when he said, "Jesus Christ...made Himself of no reputation, taking the form of a bondservant...He humbled Himself" (Philippians 2:5-8, NKJV). How could Jesus humble Himself and become a man before He was born? The answer to this question is this: Before He was born of Mary His name was already Jesus! Isaiah could not disclose the name of Jesus because God did not reveal it to him; and, God did not reveal it to Isaiah because it was not time to reveal salvation. According to Reverend David K. Bernard, "Jesus means Jehovah-Savior, Jehovah our Salvation, or Jehovah is Salvation" (Bernard, 2001). I will not elaborate or revisit the research performed by Reverend Bernard to support this conclusion, but simply say that the name of Jesus is inextricably linked with salvation! Salvation is not possible except through the death of the Lamb of God, the man Christ Jesus!

> For unto us a Child is born, Unto us a Son is given; And the government will be upon His shoulder. And His name will be called Wonderful, Counselor, Mighty God, Everlasting Father, Prince of Peace. (Isaiah 9:6, NKJV)

> And behold, you will conceive in your womb and bring forth a Son, and shall call His name Jesus. He will be great, and will be called the Son of the Highest; and the Lord God will give Him the throne of His father David. And He will reign over the house of Jacob forever, and of His kingdom there will be no end. (Luke 1:31-33, NKJV)

Isaiah's prophecy proclaimed that God Himself would dwell among men in the form of a human man, which was later reiterated to Mary by an angel (Isaiah 9:6, NKJV). In this verse, he foretold that the child born to Mary would be the "Mighty God" and "Everlasting Father." There is only one God that is mighty, and there is only one Father that is everlasting! The Almighty God has no beginning nor will He have an end! Isaiah told us a child would be born and He would be God! The

Kingdom of God has always been and will always be ruled by God Himself!

> And Jesus came and spoke to them, saying,
> All authority has been given to Me in
> heaven and on earth. Go therefore and
> make disciples of all the nations, baptizing
> them in the name of the Father and of the
> Son and of the Holy Spirit, teaching them
> to observe all things that I have
> commanded you; and lo, I am with you
> always, even to the end of the age. Amen.
> (Matthew 28:18-20, NKJV)
>
> If you love Me, keep My commandments.
> And I will pray the Father, and He will give
> you another Helper, that He may abide
> with you forever— the Spirit of truth,
> whom the world cannot receive, because it
> neither sees Him nor knows Him; but you
> know Him, for He dwells with you and will
> be in you. I will not leave you orphans; I
> will come to you. (John 14:15-18, NKJV)

Any display that God creates for Himself should not have a unique name; after all, a multitude of manifestations still only represent a single God! A unique name was not given to the fire, cloud, or hand of God, so why would any other manifestation have a different name? All manifestations of God retain the name of God, which is Jesus. As we discussed earlier, Jesus explained this concept by revealing to us the name of the Almighty God, the name of the man born to Mary, and the name of the Holy Spirit; each name is identical, they are all Jesus (Matthew 28:18-20, NKJV).

Manifestations do not change God; God uses diverse manifestations! Here Jesus confirms that He has the full power of God because He is God; therefore, He commands that we baptize in His name! He confirmed that He would remain with us even after His resurrection by saying, "I am with you always, even to the end of the age" (Matthew 28:20, NKJV). We know that Jesus remains with us today in the form of a manifestation known as the Holy Spirit. As we pointed out before, this new manifestation is not a new God! The Holy Spirit is what Jesus referred to as "another Helper" (John 14:16, NKJV). We see that Jesus dwelt with His disciples and promised to dwell inside of them (John 14:17-18, NKJV). Jesus will continue to dwell with mankind until the end of this age and He will accomplish this through the Holy Spirit!

The Gateway to God

> For the promise is to you and to your
> children, and to all who are afar off, as
> many as the Lord our God will call. (Acts
> 2:39, NKJV)

> Let us therefore come boldly to the throne
> of grace, that we may obtain mercy and
> find grace to help in time of need.
> (Hebrews 4:16, NKJV)

> Ask, and it will be given to you; seek, and
> you will find; knock, and it will be opened
> to you. For everyone who asks receives,
> and he who seeks finds, and to him who
> knocks it will be opened. (Matthew 7:7-8,
> NKJV)

Not only will Jesus dwell in His disciples, but Peter explained that the promise applies to everyone that will ever be born from the time the Holy Spirit was made available until He returns to earth! Jesus informed us that the Helper cannot be received by people that do not know Him, but the Helper will only dwell in us if we keep His commandments (John 14:15-18, NKJV). John tells us, "The world cannot receive, because it neither sees Him nor knows Him" (John 14:17, NKJV). Reading the Word of God is essential to knowing Jesus! It is the only way to know how to love Him because loving Him requires us to keep His commandments! The Bible gives multiple alternate titles for the Spirit of God; it is sometimes called the Helper, the Spirit of Truth, the Holy Ghost, or the Holy Spirit. Each title refers to the same Spirit of God. As we discussed in the last paragraph, Jesus remains with us today in the form of a new manifestation known as the Holy Spirit. To elaborate upon this point, God's Spirit did not change, but the availability of God's Spirit did change. Once Jesus Christ fulfilled His destiny and died at Calvary, people were granted access to approach the Spirit of God!

In the Old Testament, people did not have freedom to approach God; instead, they had to ask priests to facilitate their prayer and praise to God. However, that has all changed; today we can boldly approach God and present our needs to Him! We should "come boldly to the throne of grace, that we may obtain mercy" (Hebrews 4:16, NKJV). In order for us to obtain mercy, we must approach God's throne and directly ask for it! We now have an open opportunity to approach God in prayer; addressing Him in the name of Jesus because this name is the only way, or means by which, we access God. As we spoke before, this is because God's name is Jesus! Matthew informs us to "ask...seek, and...knock...For everyone who asks receives, and he who seeks finds, and to him who knocks it will be opened" (Matthew 7:7-8, NKJV). We do not have to rely on anyone else to access God on our behalf; it is our personal responsibility and privilege to obtain mercy! Mercy is a gift that can be received freely if we will approach our God and ask for it!

> For if you live according to the flesh you will die; but if by the Spirit you put to death the deeds of the body, you will live. For as many as are led by the Spirit of God, these are sons of God. For you did not receive the spirit of bondage again to fear, but you received the Spirit of adoption by whom we cry out, Abba, Father. The Spirit Himself bears witness with our spirit that we are children of God, and if children, then heirs—heirs of God and joint heirs with Christ, if indeed we suffer with Him, that we may also be glorified together. (Romans 8:13-17, NKJV)

This way to God was made available by the death of Jesus Christ; the only gateway to God! In order to take advantage of this opportunity, we must have the name of Jesus applied to our lives; we must be adopted into that name! Jesus inherited His name from God along with the Spirit of God; we also receive His name and become joint-heirs with Christ when the Spirit of God enters into our bodies.

While we are alive on this earth, we have a mortal body; however, once Christ returns, our bodies will be changed. Our mortal skin, bone, and muscle will become immortal, which means it does not have a lifespan. Our outer shell will be transformed from a body capable of death and decay to an eternal body that will never die! This is an extremely important concept to grasp! We will not exist in eternity as a spirit; we will have physical bodies! Our earthly bodies will change when Christ returns; they will transform into new physical bodies that are not capable of death or corruption. This concept is critical because we need this knowledge in order to understand Jesus Christ! Jesus Christ is still living as a human at this very moment!

> Most assuredly, I say to you, he who
> believes in Me, the works that I do he will
> do also; and greater works than these he
> will do, because I go to My Father. And
> whatever you ask in My name, that I will

do, that the Father may be glorified in the
Son. If you ask anything in My name, I will
do it. (John 14:12, NKJV)

When Jesus' mortal body died, it was transformed into an incorruptible body and was resurrected. He ascended to heaven where He continues to be the face of God! He was the face of God on earth and continues to be the face of God in heaven! God will continue to be a Spirit, just as He always has been, and He will continue to manifest Himself to us, the angels, and all of creation in the tangible body of Jesus Christ! This means that even though Jesus' Spirit is God, His body was and still is human. Before Jesus was crucified, He wielded the power of God because the Spirit of God dwelt within Him. When He healed the sick and raised the dead, it was a result of God's power. This is great news to all of us because He promised that anyone that has the Spirit of God can also perform the same miracles! In fact, He said it is through His power that we will perform even greater miracles than He did when He was on earth in human form!

During a minister's meeting in early 2020, Reverend David Beecham explained that the "greater works" is that of quantity and not quality (John 14:12, NKJV). We do the same miraculous works as Jesus, but it is magnified due to an influx in instances, which is a result of a greater population of Spirit filled people. Each person is being used as a conduit through which God's Spirit flows and works. If we are filled with the Spirit of God, we have the same power Jesus had when He walked on earth because it is the same Spirit that fills us!

It was the Spirit of God that enabled Jesus to perform miracles. We discussed earlier how we are adopted into the family of God when we are filled with the Holy Spirit. Jesus tells us that we will perform miracles by praying in His name. Anyone who receives the Spirit of God can wield the power of God through the name of Jesus! Why would calling upon the name of Jesus initiate a response from the Spirit of God? Because God's name is Jesus and He responds to His name!

There is one work that Jesus performed while He walked on this earth that people will never be able to perform. During His earthly life, Jesus had the power to forgive sin (Matthew 9:1-7, KJV). When Jesus encountered people in need, He was inclined to help. A person with faith that needed forgiveness was just as eligible as a person that needed any other miracle. It is important to remember that before Jesus' death, salvation was not available to mankind. This is why Jesus forgave sin while he was on earth; salvation had not yet been made available. Even after being filled with the Spirit of God, we do not have authority to forgive sin because, through His death, Jesus provided a specific prescription for salvation! If a medical doctor writes you a prescription for an antibiotic, the pharmacy should not sell you a pain reliever! After Christ's death, a path of salvation was prescribed, and there is no generic substitute or alternative! When Jesus told His disciples that sin cannot be remitted without their efforts, He was conveying the massive responsibility associated with working in God's Kingdom (John 20:23, KJV). We cannot forgive sin, but sin will not be forgiven without preaching, teaching, loving, and facilitating Christ to our world! Through Jesus' death, resurrection, and glorification, He established a pathway to salvation. He gave us specific orders on how we should prepare our temple in order to be filled with the Holy Spirit, and this new pathway is the only method of procuring salvation! Only Christ has the power and authority to judge mankind; therefore, He alone can forgive sin, we do not possess that power (Revelation 20:11-12, NKJV). However, as we mentioned before, the miraculous healings, deliverances, and blessings are accessible by those filled with the Spirit of God!

Once we are adopted into the family of God, the Spirit of God gives us power to perform the same miracles that Jesus Christ performed while He was on earth! Blind eyes can be opened, deaf ears can hear, the lame can walk, the dead can be raised to life and all manner of miracles can be performed!

Jesus says if we pray in His name, He will answer our prayers! He said, "And whatever you ask in My name, that I will do, that the Father may be glorified in the Son" (John 14:12, NKJV). When prayers are answered, God receives glory through Jesus! Since God is all-powerful, how does He receive glory when Jesus performs miracles? God does not allow Jesus Christ to borrow some of His power and then take credit for the miracles! This would violate everything we know about God! God gets the credit for miracles because His name is Jesus!

God's Throne

> And the Lord shall be King over all the earth. In that day it shall be—The Lord is one, And His name one. (Zechariah 14:9, NKJV)

The last chapter in the book of Zechariah is prophetic in nature and concerns the return of the Messiah; when this chapter discusses the Lord ruling over all the earth, it is talking about Christ. God is going to establish a Kingdom here on earth, and Jesus Christ will be the King over this empire (Zechariah 14:9, NKJV). The prophecy we just read tells us that God Himself is going to be the King! This Old Testament prophet is trying to explain that Jesus is not just the name of the Christ, but also the name of God. He is telling us that there is no distinction between God and Christ; both are the same entity! The human King is the face of Almighty God! There is only one Lord and Jesus is His name!

> But now Christ is risen from the dead, and has become the firstfruits of those who have fallen asleep. (1 Corinthians 15:20, NKJV)

The new immortal body of Jesus is a real, physical body. Once He returns to earth, we will be able to see and touch Him! One day our physical bodies will also be transformed, and they will have the same characteristics as Jesus' current body. We know this because we will be given immortal bodies just prior to Christ's Kingdom, and we will rule alongside Jesus Christ for one thousand years. The similarities between our new bodies and Jesus' current body were confirmed when Paul said that Jesus is the "firstfruits" of the resurrection (1 Corinthians 15:20, NKJV). This literally means we will be transformed and resurrected the same as Jesus Christ! Jesus was the first to be resurrected and our resurrection will be the completion of that resurrection. If we have the same Holy

Spirit residing in us, we will receive the same body at our resurrection that He received!

> And I looked, and behold, in the midst of the throne and of the four living creatures, and in the midst of the elders, stood a Lamb as though it had been slain, having seven horns and seven eyes, which are the seven Spirits of God sent out into all the earth. (Revelation 5:6, NKJV)

> Saying with a loud voice: Worthy is the Lamb who was slain To receive power and riches and wisdom, And strength and honor and glory and blessing! And every creature which is in heaven and on the earth and under the earth and such as are in the sea, and all that are in them, I heard saying: Blessing and honor and glory and power Be to Him who sits on the throne, And to the Lamb, forever and ever! (Revelation 5:12-13, NKJV)

> And when I saw Him, I fell at His feet as dead. But He laid His right hand on me, saying to me, Do not be afraid; I am the

First and the Last. I am He who lives, and
was dead, and behold, I am alive
forevermore. Amen. And I have the keys of
Hades and of Death. (Revelation 1:17-18,
NKJV)

The Book of Revelation is a revealing of Jesus Christ
(Revelation 1:1, KJV). We see that Jesus Christ began sitting on
the throne after He ascended into heaven! The "Lamb as
though it had been slain" is a metaphor for Jesus Christ; it
references His crucifixion (Revelation 5:6, NKJV). Jesus Christ
has all power, riches, wisdom, strength, honor, and glory,
which will be verbalized by every human being in heaven and
earth as they praise Him (Revelation 5:12-13, NKJV). How long
is Jesus Christ going to be worthy of such praise? We see that
this praise is given "to the Lamb, forever and ever" (Revelation
5:13, NKJV). A man that sits on the throne of God had better
have all power in heaven and earth, and, as we read earlier,
Jesus Christ is the man with this kind of power (Matthew
28:18, NKJV). Furthermore, only God can claim to be the first
and the last because only God predates birth and will never
decease! We see that it is Jesus Christ speaking because He
says He lived, died, and was resurrected, and, since a spirit

cannot die, it must be the human Messiah speaking to John (Revelation 1:17-18, NKJV).

Only one Man has the right to claim to be both eternal and also experience death and resurrection! John revealed to us that Jesus Christ is both the eternal God and the Messiah; Jesus Christ said, "I am alive forevermore" (Revelation 1:18, NKJV). How can any human be bold enough to sit on the throne of God? The only way to understand how a human will sit on the throne of God is to understand that God manifested Himself in the human form of Jesus Christ! Any other scenario would be unacceptable because we have already discussed how God is jealous of our praise and affection! God certainly would not allow such praise to an unworthy being. Jesus Christ has the authority to sit on God's throne because He is God in human form!

> Look to Me, and be saved, All you ends of the earth! For I am God, and there is no other. I have sworn by Myself; The word has gone out of My mouth in righteousness, And shall not return, That to Me every knee shall bow, Every tongue shall take an oath. (Isaiah 45:22-23, NKJV)

> Therefore God also has highly exalted Him
> and given Him the name which is above
> every name, that at the name of Jesus
> every knee should bow, of those in heaven,
> and of those on earth, and of those under
> the earth, and that every tongue should
> confess that Jesus Christ is Lord, to the
> glory of God the Father. (Philippians 2:9-
> 11, NKJV)

I recently saw a cartoon image of God sitting on His throne in heaven. In this cartoon, Jesus Christ was not the man sitting on the throne; instead, it was a being many times larger than humans. It was obvious that the being on the throne was much larger than a human because humans were also drawn in this cartoon; they were standing around God's throne. The artist was apparently attempting to depict how an Almighty God might look as He sits on His throne, but this artist lacked clear understanding of God's characteristics. The artist fell into the trap of trying to limit the Spirit of God based on humanistic ideas. John shows us that Jesus Christ is clearly the man that occupies the throne in heaven (Revelation 5:6-13, NKJV). The Spirit of God will not have a separate throne sitting beside Jesus Christ's throne. There will be no need for a big throne beside Jesus Christ's smaller man-sized throne because the

Spirit of God does not have parameters. How large would a throne have to be on which an everywhere God would sit? If Solomon could not build a house large enough to contain God, how will any throne contain Him? The answer is clear, there will be only one throne and Jesus Christ will sit upon it as Almighty God! There is a reason the name of Jesus is greater than any other name; there is a reason all power in heaven and earth belongs to Jesus! It is not a sharing arrangement, and Jesus did not steal God's power! God still retains all power; the only difference is His name has been revealed!

We will finish this chapter out with a passage we discussed earlier. Isaiah prophesied that every knee would bow to God; Paul referenced this prophecy except he applied it to Jesus Christ (Philippians 2:5-11, NKJV). In this passage, Paul said, "God...has highly exalted Him and given Him the name which is above every name, that at the name of Jesus every knee should bow." One day we will stand in God's presence and talk with Him face to face. We will be able to witness His glory as we stand before His throne! We will all gather and worship Him as our King! God has a human body, which is the Lamb of God slain for the sins of all mankind! One day we will be able to look into the eyes of God; we will be able to physically see the God of all creation. The face on which we look will be that of Jesus Christ; His face is the face of Almighty God!

FOUR

Seeing Through Glass Brightly!

Drawing Conclusions

In chapter two, we discussed the Spirit of God and His deity. Chapter three explained how Jesus Christ is the expression, or manifestation, of the Spirit of God. At this point, we should be able to easily distinguish between God's Spirit and any physical form He chooses to take. In chapter one, we spoke about performing a proverbial litmus test; we were analyzing scripture in order to determine whether or not the Bible supports the concept of God displaying Himself in human form. This is exactly what we want to do in this chapter! We will test what we have learned to see if it holds up under scrutiny, and we will attempt to clear up any confusion that may still exist. Was Jesus fully human or did He have some pseudo-human experience? Did God really exist in two different locations at once? Do Jesus and God really have different personalities? We will try to answer these questions and possibly others as we work our way through this chapter. We will focus primarily on Bible verses that are often misunderstood or misinterpreted.

Sometimes we draw the wrong conclusion when we look at one or two verses without considering everything else the Bible has to say on any particular subject. It reminds me of a story I once heard about a group of blind men that encountered an elephant for the first time. One man felt of the elephant's trunk and declared: An elephant is like a snake. Another man felt of the elephant's ear and proclaimed: An elephant is like a fan. A third man felt of the elephant's leg and exclaimed: An elephant is like a tree. Each man's encounter with the elephant led to a different conclusion, but the elephant did not change. God may look very different depending on the portion of the Bible that is considered. It is important for us to look at the whole Bible in order to fully understand the nature and characteristics of God before drawing a conclusion. If you do not understand God, you will never understand how He works or reveals Himself. A global approach is even more important when we try to understand Jesus, and it becomes absolutely critical when we try to reconcile our knowledge of Jesus against our knowledge of God. For instance, if we only read the verse talking about Jesus' birth to Mary, we could rightfully conclude that Jesus is a very special man. However, that is not a complete assessment of Jesus! Furthermore, if we read only the verses where all people bow their knee before Jesus confessing that He is Lord of heaven and earth, we could rightfully conclude that Jesus is supernatural and supremely divine. Both of these conclusions are correct based on the limited assessment of Jesus, but neither tells the full story! When we take a bird's eye view of all scripture, we see the Spirit of Almighty God that has been displayed through many manifestations throughout the millennia. Most recently He is being displayed through the human body of Jesus Christ. You cannot overlook that Jesus is human, and you cannot discount that He is God. One without the other is only a partial story!

The Test Continued

> Jesus spoke these words, lifted up His eyes
> to heaven, and said: Father, the hour has
> come. Glorify Your Son, that Your Son also
> may glorify You. (John 17:1, NKJV)

One scenario that seems to thoroughly confuse people is when Jesus prays to God. It does not make logical sense to us that God can pray to Himself, so how do we interpret this verse? In order to take a bird's eye view, the timeframe of the scenario is critical; we must consider: Did it take place prior to or after Christ died on the cross? Answering this question is critical to arriving at the proper interpretation. John gives us Jesus' opening lines of a prayer to God just before He is betrayed by Judas (John 17:1, NKJV). In this verse, Jesus prayed, "Father, the hour has come. Glorify Your Son," this prayer was prayed before He was crucified. This verse uses the word "glorify," which means to render glorious or to make honorable (Strong, Doxazo Meaning in Bible - New Testament Greek Lexicon - King James Version 1890). Before Jesus' death, He lacked glory; He was humble, limited in knowledge and mental capacity, and weak in body. However, after Jesus' death, we see He has all power in heaven and earth, and He is not limited in any way!

> These things I have spoken to you in figurative language; but the time is coming when I will no longer speak to you in figurative language, but I will tell you plainly about the Father. In that day you will ask in My name, and I do not say to you that I shall pray the Father for you; for the Father Himself loves you, because you have loved Me, and have believed that I

came forth from God. I came forth from the Father and have come into the world. Again, I leave the world and go to the Father. (John 16:25-28, NKJV)

Then Jesus, when He had found a young donkey, sat on it; as it is written: Fear not, daughter of Zion; Behold, your King is coming, Sitting on a donkey's colt. His disciples did not understand these things at first; but when Jesus was glorified, then they remembered that these things were written about Him and that they had done these things to Him. (John 12:14-16, NKJV)

He who believes in Me, as the Scripture has said, out of his heart will flow rivers of living water. But this He spoke concerning the Spirit, whom those believing in Him would receive; for the Holy Spirit was not yet given, because Jesus was not yet glorified. (John 7:38-39, NKJV)

The twenty-four elders fall down before Him who sits on the throne and worship Him who lives forever and ever, and cast their crowns before the throne, saying: You

are worthy, O Lord, To receive glory and
honor and power; For You created all
things, And by Your will they exist and
were created. (Revelation 4:10-11, NKJV)

What changed at Jesus' death? When we see verses about
Jesus being glorified it is talking about His transformation from
a lowly human back into the lofty God! After death, Jesus'
limitations and restrictions were removed! He went from
weakness to having all strength! He changed from having
mental limitations to possessing all knowledge! After Jesus
overcame sin, there was no need for Him to retain His human
limitations. He simply returned to His former all-powerful
state! When Jesus said, "I came forth from the Father," He was
not talking about taking a hiatus from God's company in order
to do some traveling around earth (John 16:28, NKJV). No,
Jesus is talking about being a created manifestation of God,
and, after death, He was glorified as the body of God!

The term *glorified* is quite vague, so what does the Bible
mean when it says Jesus was glorified? John spells it out clearly
when he says, "You are worthy, O Lord, To receive glory and
honor and power; For You created all things, And by Your will
they exist and were created" (Revelation 4:11, NKJV). John
really does not leave any loose ends untied with his statement!

Notice that Jesus spoke in figurative language while here on earth, but, afterwards, no longer taught in proverbs and ceased praying to God (John 16:25, NKJV). Instead, people pray in Jesus name, and it is Jesus who responds to prayer! Jesus is, at this very moment, receiving this kind of treatment in heaven! The King is sitting on His throne and worship is going forth around His throne! This takes all of the ambiguity out of what it means to be glorified! The shackles of humanity fell from Jesus after His death, and He took His place on the throne of heaven!

We get a picture of Jesus as an earthly man before He was glorified (John 17:1, NKJV). Jesus is fully human, which brings with it every limitation that you and I experience. As a man, the only way Jesus was able to have knowledge of the future was through: studying the Jewish Tanakh, listening to stories passed down from His elders, and having the Spirit of God reveal truth to Him. In case you are unfamiliar with the Jewish Tanakh, it contains the same books of the Bible that make up the Old Testament. Receiving revelation from the Spirit requires prayer, so Jesus undoubtedly spent much time in prayer! It was the knowledge that Jesus acquired and His faith that kept Him on the path to the cross in order to fulfill His purpose in dying for all mankind! Jesus prayed in His human flesh because He was weak and needed help from the Spirit of

God! We all should learn from His example! We are at our weakest when we do not know God's word and become lackadaisical in our prayer life. We should study God's word, build our faith, and pray in our weakest moments! This weakness of flesh was also experienced by Jesus; He had to remain vigilant in His study and consistent in His prayer life in order to overcome His flesh! Jesus is the perfect example of how we should live our lives!

To elaborate upon a point made earlier, we must remember that we have both a spirit and a body. We as humans are not acutely aware of our spirit, but we are absolutely aware of our bodies. We know our spirit exists and has eternal significance, but we view ourselves through an earthly lens, which is overwhelmingly focused on the natural body. We have a tendency to gravitate towards what can be seen, felt, smelt, tasted, or heard. Following after a spiritual desire does not come naturally to us. Jesus was just like this, He had knowledge of His role in God's plan, but He had to pray for strength in order to fulfill that role! It is through prayer that we resist our physical desires, and hone in on spiritual needs. At our core, we have a basic awareness of right and wrong, but our human flesh is weak; it loves to take us down the wrong path.

Our flesh does not enjoy obeying God's will for our lives. Jesus never disobeyed the Holy Spirit during His life on earth. Even though Jesus avoided all sin, He was still a man that saw through His natural human eyes, thought using His human brain, and spoke through His human mouth. Jesus needed to pray as much as any of us need to pray! We can hardly make it through one day without failing God in one way or another; Jesus remains the only perfect human to ever live on earth! I am not at all surprised to see evidence of Jesus' passionate, authentic prayer life! It is the only way He managed to win the battle against His flesh and overcome sin!

> As You have given Him authority over all flesh, that He should give eternal life to as many as You have given Him. And this is eternal life, that they may know You, the only true God, and Jesus Christ whom You have sent. I have glorified You on the earth. I have finished the work which You have given Me to do. And now, O Father, glorify Me together with Yourself, with the glory which I had with You before the world was. (John 17:2-5, NKJV)

Here we see a continuation of the prayer we discussed earlier in this chapter. In this passage of the Bible, Jesus asks God to resurrect Him and change His body from mortal to immortality. We have already discussed why Jesus prayed, and that Jesus was the first fruit, or initial participant, of the resurrection. In His human prayer, Jesus exclaimed that He completed His earthly ministry and was ready for eternal life. This is another example of Jesus Christ praying to God, which can be confusing for those that do not understand the relationship between Christ and God. We have already covered this previously, but will summarize it briefly. At this point in time, Jesus was aware that His Spirit is the Spirit of God, which will enable Him to live forever as Lord of Lords; however, Jesus' journey and destination were two very different realities! The mortal Jesus needed help that the immortal Jesus no longer requires! While Jesus had knowledge of the prophecies that proclaim Him to be the Almighty God, His flesh was undoubtedly experiencing temptation at that very moment! Jesus repeated a prayer that He likely prayed many times before that moment. He was simply getting His flesh into alignment with the Spirit of God, and He was ensuring that He stayed on the right path. Jesus prayed, "Glorify Me together with Yourself, with the glory which I had with You before the world was" (John 17:5, NKJV). He prayed a prayer to build His human faith. He did not ask for something that was outside of the plan; He simply prayed Himself into alignment with the plan!

When we see Jesus pray, we are able to see that Jesus knew His potential, but yet He still prays for help! Again, Jesus' request was to be glorified with the glory that He possessed before the world was created (John 17:5, NKJV). Jesus was aware that His Spirit was the very Spirit of God, but at that moment His carnal flesh was weighing Him down! He still required prayer in order to help put His humanity under subjection and fulfill God's will for His life! What an absolutely perfect example of what we should do each and every day. This is why God placed Himself in such a weak and vulnerable position; in order to show us how to respond! He gave us a perfect example to follow! Our carnal flesh is constantly warring against our spirit, and, in order to fulfill God's will for our lives, we must follow Jesus' example and seek His help!

John solidified Jesus' deity by saying, "That He [Jesus] should give eternal life to as many as You have given Him…And this is eternal life, that they may know You, the only true God, and Jesus Christ whom You have sent" (John 17:3, NKJV). If the God to which Jesus prayed is the only true God, why does Jesus have authority to grant eternal life? Furthermore, if eternal life is knowing God and Jesus Christ, how do we know them? We can only know the true Almighty God by having a relationship with Jesus Christ! Jesus said, "I am the way, the truth, and the life. No one comes to the Father except through Me" (John 14:6, NKJV). We can obtain eternal life through Jesus Christ, which is our only path to knowing the true God! We will discuss this path in greater detail later in chapter five and six of this book.

> But of that day and hour no one knows, not even the angels in heaven, nor the Son, but only the Father. (Mark 13:32, NKJV)

> Then Jesus answered and said to them, Most assuredly, I say to you, the Son can do nothing of Himself, but what He sees the Father do; for whatever He does, the Son also does in like manner. (John 5:19, NKJV)

> Then Jesus said to them, When you lift up the Son of Man, then you will know that I am He, and that I do nothing of Myself; but as My Father taught Me, I speak these things. (John 8:28, NKJV)

Here we see a few potentially tricky verses. We see that Jesus had limited knowledge of the future, and His power and teaching ability was limited by what He learned from the Holy Spirit. While on earth, Jesus readily admitted to having limitations. Most of the time, He referred to Himself as the Son of man as opposed to the Son of God, which means He acknowledged His weakness. These verses further prove that Jesus was fully human and not some pseudo-human. Jesus was in the identical predicament that you and I find ourselves in today, which is important because He had to prove to us that we can accomplish what He has accomplished! He proved to us that we can overcome sin! If Jesus did not have the same weaknesses that plague each of us, His sacrifice would not offer us hope. If He walked a different path than what we are forced to travel, His journey would not be an example for us to follow! However, we are able to know the way to salvation because Jesus has already traveled our road, and He left us a roadmap that leads to treasures in heaven! The cross of Calvary is the proverbial X that marks the spot on our Biblical treasure map to eternal life!

> And he hewed two tables of stone like
> unto the first; and Moses rose up early in
> the morning, and went up unto mount

Sinai, as the Lord had commanded him, and took in his hand the two tables of stone. And the Lord descended in the cloud, and stood with him there, and proclaimed the name of the Lord. And the Lord passed by before him, and proclaimed, The Lord, The Lord God, merciful and gracious, longsuffering, and abundant in goodness and truth. (Exodus 34:4-6, KJV)

It came to pass in those days that Jesus came from Nazareth of Galilee, and was baptized by John in the Jordan. And immediately, coming up from the water, He saw the heavens parting and the Spirit descending upon Him like a dove. Then a voice came from heaven, You are My beloved Son, in whom I am well pleased. (Mark 1:9-11, NKJV)

And the angel of God, which went before the camp of Israel, removed and went behind them; and the pillar of the cloud went from before their face, and stood behind them: And it came between the

camp of the Egyptians and the camp of
Israel; and it was a cloud and darkness to
them, but it gave light by night to these: so
that the one came not near the other all
the night. (Exodus 14:19-20, KJV)

And so it is written, The first man Adam
became a living being. The last Adam
became a life-giving spirit. However, the
spiritual is not first, but the natural, and
afterward the spiritual. The first man was
of the earth, made of dust; the second
Man is the Lord from heaven. (1
Corinthians 15:45-47, NKJV)

You might wonder and I have heard in the past: How can
Jesus have His own personality if He and God are the same
entity? The answer is that Jesus Christ was limited in power,
knowledge, and physical location while He was on earth in His
mortal state; the Spirit of God has never been and never will be
limited by any of these factors. Remember that God can never
have limitations because He is limitless! With God, all things
are possible! God can express Himself in two or more
simultaneous manifestations without violating the Hebrew
Shema (the Lord is one)!

An example of an instance where God maintained two simultaneous manifestations can be found in Exodus 34. In the wilderness, the Israelites saw God as a cloud around Mount Sinai, but God was something completely different when He passed by Moses (Exodus 34:5-6, KJV). Did God stop being the cloud while He revealed Himself in another form to Moses? No, He was two simultaneous manifestations at once! What about when God's voice came from heaven while He descended upon Jesus after He was baptized? When Jesus was baptized, God was an audible voice, a dove, a man, and an omnipresent Spirit all at once (Mark 1:9-11, NKJV). Moses described God's dual, simultaneous physical display as being a dark cloud to the Egyptians while giving light to the Hebrews (Exodus 14:19-20, KJV). How can God continue to be a Spirit, a dark cloud, and a light? It is because God is limitless! Multiple manifestations of God do not equal multiple Gods. It just means God is representing Himself in multiple ways! A conversation between a limitless Spirit of God and a limited manifestation of God does not mean that God has multiple personalities. Jesus' human flesh gave Him fleshly desires, but His Spirit was and still is the Spirit of God! Adam received life from God, but, when Jesus was formed, He became the life giver (1 Corinthians 15:45, NKJV). Only the Spirit of God is capable of giving life!

Paul said, "The second Man is the Lord from heaven" (1 Corinthians 15:47, NKJV). He tells us that Jesus Christ is unequivocally the Lord from heaven! Jesus Christ was not a Lord or part of the Lord; Jesus Christ is simply the same Lord that exists in heaven! This is important because if God never changes, and Jesus Christ is God, then the body of Jesus Christ must be an expression of God's Spirit! The only viable explanation is that the human Christ is a mechanism God uses to facilitate communication between Himself and His creation! Earlier in this chapter, we discussed how it is important to analyze whether a scenario occurred before or after Christ's death. All conversation between God and Jesus occurred prior to the crucifixion. Before the crucifixion, Jesus was plagued by His human flesh, but, after His crucifixion, He was freed from His limitations and released to be the Lord God of heaven!

God can exist in His Spirit state as well as manifest Himself as a man on earth at the same time. God knows the end from the beginning, but the limited Messiah needed an opportunity to be fully human. The Messiah could only be fully human if He restricted His knowledge, power, and location! This means He had to reduce Himself to a mortal state, which we discussed in chapter three; Paul recorded that Jesus "humbled Himself and became obedient to the point of death, even the death of the cross" (Philippians 2:8, NKJV). In order to become human, the

Almighty God had to limit His power and restrict His limitless abilities! Jesus had to be completely human in order to be able to grow and learn. How can a God that already knows everything and exists everywhere grow and learn? This is where the manifestation comes into the picture.

Jesus had to have the same human experience that each of us live every single day. He had to start with human limitations and grow into spiritual maturity as the Spirit of God trained Him! Otherwise, He would not be our perfect example. How would we know that success is possible unless a man showed us how to succeed? Jesus showed all of mankind how to be the men and women that God designed us to be! We were not designed to be separated from God by sin! We were designed to be in perfect relationship with God, and, because of Jesus' example, we now know how to accomplish relationship with Him!

> And I saw in the right hand of Him who sat on the throne a scroll written inside and on the back, sealed with seven seals. Then I saw a strong angel proclaiming with a loud voice, Who is worthy to open the scroll and to loose its seals? And no one in heaven or on the earth or under the earth was able to open the scroll, or to look at it. So I wept

much, because no one was found worthy
to open and read the scroll, or to look at
it. But one of the elders said to me, Do not
weep. Behold, the Lion of the tribe
of Judah, the Root of David, has prevailed
to open the scroll and to loose its seven
seals. And I looked, and behold, in the
midst of the throne and of the four living
creatures, and in the midst of the elders,
stood a Lamb as though it had been slain,
having seven horns and seven eyes, which
are the seven Spirits of God sent out into
all the earth. Then He came and took the
scroll out of the right hand of Him who sat
on the throne. Now when He had taken
the scroll, the four living creatures and the
twenty-four elders fell down before the
Lamb, each having a harp, and golden
bowls full of incense, which are the prayers
of the saints. And they sang a new song,
saying: You are worthy to take the scroll,
And to open its seals; For You were slain,
And have redeemed us to God by Your
blood Out of every tribe and tongue and
people and nation, And have
made us kings and priests to our God;

And we shall reign on the earth. Then I
looked, and I heard the voice of many
angels around the throne, the living
creatures, and the elders; and the number
of them was ten thousand times ten
thousand, and thousands of
thousands, saying with a loud voice:
Worthy is the Lamb who was slain To
receive power and riches and wisdom,
And strength and honor and glory and
blessing! And every creature which is in
heaven and on the earth and under the
earth and such as are in the sea, and all
that are in them, I heard saying: Blessing
and honor and glory and power Be to
Him who sits on the throne, And to the
Lamb, forever and ever! Then the four
living creatures said, Amen! And
the twenty-four elders fell down and
worshiped Him who lives forever and ever.
(Revelation 5:1-14, NKJV)

The book of Revelation can be more difficult to understand
than other books of the Bible, but it is by no means impossible!
The fifth chapter of Revelation definitely falls into this
category; it requires careful consideration, analysis, and

thought in order to understand. A few obvious questions arise after reading this chapter. Who is the slain Lamb with seven horns and seven eyes that was worthy to open the book? Who was the one on the throne that was unworthy to open the book? Did the one that previously inhabited the throne abdicate in order to allow the Lamb to sit on the throne forever? We will discuss and answer these questions.

First, it is important to understand the context of this chapter. John had this vision while he was imprisoned on the isle of Patmos. As John reveals in chapter one, the purpose for the book of Revelation is to reveal Jesus Christ. This means that all twenty-two chapters in the book of Revelation relate to Jesus Christ. We know that Jesus did not have seven horns and seven eyes, but the Lamb in this book is obviously a metaphor for Jesus Christ. We know this because Jesus Christ is described as a lamb in several other passages in the Bible. This leads us to our next question: Who was on the throne in heaven that was unworthy to open the book?

Since the throne is in heaven, it would not be considered speculation to say the occupant of the throne is God. After all, God is the Almighty, and, without a doubt, He is the One we expect to rule heaven with authority! So if God inhabited the throne in the beginning of John's vision, the perplexing part is why was God unworthy to open the book? John said, "Then I saw a strong angel proclaiming with a loud voice, Who is worthy to open the scroll and to loose its seals? And no one in heaven or on the earth or under the earth was able to open the scroll, or to look at it" (Revelation 5:2-3, NKJV). The God of everything was unworthy to open a book? This seems to contradict just about every other concept found in the Word of God! In fact, we just spent the first two chapters of this book detailing God's power, authority, and mighty characteristics! If anyone is worthy to open a book, it should definitely be the supreme God of heaven! However, we see here that only Jesus Christ was worthy to open the book (Baxter, 2020).

Our third question deals with: Who will forever occupy the throne in heaven? At the beginning of the vision, the throne was occupied by God, but halfway through John's vision the throne began to be occupied with Jesus Christ! So not only did Jesus Christ take the book from God, but He also took the throne? The answer is not quite as scandalous as it appears! John is not describing a coup that takes place between Jesus Christ and God; neither is it a transition of power between God and Jesus Christ. Instead, what we see here is a vision that explains the necessity for God to come to earth as a human being.

God had to go through the human experience, take on the limitations of human flesh, and win the battle over sin! Irvin

Baxter states, "Until Almighty God came to earth as the Lamb, and was tempted in all points like as we are, He was not worthy to unleash the judgments upon the earth...to open the seals of the book. This was not one God taking the book out of the right hand of another God...This is a picture of Almighty God becoming man...and then qualifying...[Himself] to judge fairly"(Baxter, 2020). God did not want to judge mankind until He experienced what mankind experiences! John wrote, "For You were slain, and have redeemed us to God by Your blood" (Revelation 5:9, NKJV). God has never lost nor will He ever lose His supremacy; He only expanded our access to Him by becoming a human being and dying for our sins! It was God's own blood, or the blood of Jesus Christ, that redeemed us back to God! John's vision was figurative in nature, not literal. A physical God will not give up His position to Jesus Christ because God is a Spirit. As we discussed earlier in this book, the fullness of the Godhead resides in the body of Jesus Christ. God will rule heaven and earth through the body of Jesus Christ!

> And they heard the voice of the Lord God
> walking in the garden in the cool of the
> day: and Adam and his wife hid themselves
> from the presence of the Lord God

amongst the trees of the garden. (Genesis
3:8, KJV)

The human Jesus, acting as the face of God, is similar to a
computer acting as the interaction point between a human and
the internet. For instance, a person would be unable to access
the internet and its vast amount of data content without a
tablet or computer to help facilitate this exchange. This is
similar to how we communicate with God; without
manifestations we would have no access to Him. The data of
the internet by itself has vast potential; however, without a
computer and supporting software, the data could not be seen
or heard. The data still exists, but it is simply inaccessible by
humans. Similarly, without a physical manifestation of Jesus
Christ, our limitations would preclude us from communicating
with God. It was through a manifestation that God walked and
communicated with Adam and Eve in the garden. An
omnipresent God does not cease from His everywhere
existence. Instead, God utilized some physical form to walk and
converse with Adam and Eve. If a human Jesus never existed,
we would not have the unlimited access to God that we enjoy
today! It is through Jesus Christ that we have salvation, the
benefits of Spiritual adoption, and a man with whom we can
openly communicate.

Let us flesh out this analogy even further. For a moment, think of Jesus as a computer. Imagine that the Jesus computer is connected to an infinite volume of data, but, before His death, His access was restricted to a miniscule amount of this data. However, after Jesus' death, His restrictions were removed, and He gained full access to all of the data! God "humbled Himself" when He was born as a human, so it stands to reason that He exalted Himself after His death (Philippians 2:8, NKJV). In fact, according to John, this is exactly what happened (John 17:5, NKJV). A God that was humbled by human limitation was also exalted by their removal!

While Jesus was on earth, He grew from an infant into a man; during His years on earth some additional knowledge became available to Him. All throughout His life, He was taught by the Holy Spirit that resided within Him, but it was not until after Jesus died that all limitations were removed! After His death, Jesus was suddenly able to access all knowledge and all power! While He was on earth, Jesus had the same emotional, physical, and mental limitations that every other human experiences. He did not have an advantage over us because any advantage would diminish His sacrifice. Jesus had to obtain victory over sin and carnality, and He had to do it in His own human skin!

> But he, being full of the Holy Spirit, gazed
> into heaven and saw the glory of God, and
> Jesus standing at the right hand of God.
> (Acts 7:55, NKJV)

> This Jesus God has raised up, of which we
> are all witnesses. Therefore being exalted
> to the right hand of God, and having
> received from the Father the promise of
> the Holy Spirit, He poured out this which
> you now see and hear. (Acts 2:32-33, NKJV)

Another potentially confusing passage of scripture is when the Bible references the "right hand of God" (Acts 7:55, NKJV). First of all, it is important to remember that spirits do not have hands. We talked about the nature and characteristics of God in chapter one. God exists everywhere, so where would someone find His right side or right hand? Just as the omnipresent Spirit of God is not limited to any physical location, His Spirit is also not able to be limited by hands. When the Bible refers to the right hand of God, it is a metaphor for the power of God. This passage is pointing out that, after Jesus' death, He is revered in heaven as having the power of God! In Steven's vision, he saw Jesus Christ in heaven being treated as God! Earlier when we were analyzing

Revelation 5, we spoke about Jesus sitting on the throne of heaven. God and Jesus will not sit side by side, since God cannot sit, stand, or kneel. God already occupies all space everywhere. In fact, Jesus Christ and any other manifestation that God chooses to use are the only physical characteristics of God. Jesus is treated like God in heaven because He is God in human form!

Attainable Perfection

> Seeing then that we have a great High Priest who has passed through the heavens, Jesus the Son of God, let us hold fast our confession. For we do not have a High Priest who cannot sympathize with our weaknesses, but was in all points tempted as we are, yet without sin. Let us therefore come boldly to the throne of grace, that we may obtain mercy and find grace to help in time of need. (Hebrews 4:14-16, NKJV)

> By a new and living way which He consecrated for us, through the veil, that is, His flesh. (Hebrews 10:20, NKJV)

It was *through* His flesh that Jesus consecrated, or inaugurated, a path to salvation! In other words, He blazed a trail for us to follow! If Jesus was able to overcome while living a fleshly existence, we are also able to overcome living in our flesh! This is how He became our perfect sacrifice! Perfection lived out through imperfect flesh, which was made possible through a perfect Spirit! We see that Jesus is touched by our weakness because He "in all points" had the same weaknesses (Hebrews 4:15, NKJV). However, the good news of the gospel is that Jesus completed His mission! He refused to sin and became the perfect, sacrificed Lamb of God.

Perfection is not attainable in the world in which we live. Many people search and strive for it, but it is an elusive goal. In fact, not only is it hard to achieve, but many people struggle in defining it. The perfect job or the perfect life, as some may define them, would undoubtedly still be fraught with imperfections. This is because we have come to expect imperfection. We have never experienced it; therefore, we tend to lower our expectations and refer to that which is good as *perfect*. However, God defines perfect in another way. His way does not leave room for error or perception. His way raises perfect back up to meet lofty expectations!

Love never fails. But whether there are
prophecies, they will fail; whether there
are tongues, they will cease; whether there
is knowledge, it will vanish away. For we
know in part and we prophesy in part. But
when that which is perfect has come, then
that which is in part will be done away.
When I was a child, I spoke as a child, I
understood as a child, I thought as a child;
but when I became a man, I put away
childish things. For now we see in a mirror,
dimly, but then face to face. Now I know in
part, but then I shall know just as I also am
known. (1 Corinthians 13:8-12, NKJV)

Paul said, "But when that which is perfect has come" (1
Corinthians 13:10, NKJV). The only man that will ever fit the
description of perfect is Jesus Christ. He lived a sinless life and
became the ultimate sacrifice for people that do not deserve
the gift that He freely gives. Notice that the scripture refers to
knowledge and prophecy as childish. This terminology is meant
to draw a glaring distinction between how God and mankind
define *perfect*. The world and even the church place education
in high regard. People pay hundreds of thousands of dollars for
education, but we see here that having knowledge, as it exists

today, is like speaking and thinking as children! Paul summarized this phenomenon when he said we presently "see through a glass, darkly" (1 Corinthians 8:12, KJV); however, when Christ returns, we will see clearly! Paul was contrasting the state of knowledge before Jesus Christ returns against knowledge after His return. Before Christ returns, knowledge is childish, but, after He returns, knowledge will be fully mature. What we think we know and what we have been taught in school will pale in comparison to what Jesus will reveal to us!

This is how different the world will be when Jesus returns the second time! Perfection, in the true sense of the word, will not be available until His return. At His second coming, He will collect His saints, or the people who have been filled with His Holy Spirit, and they will begin to rule alongside Him in His earthly government for one thousand years. His saints will have perfect understanding! They will no longer need education, training, instruction, or tutelage! The saints will have perfect knowledge, assist Jesus Christ in managing a perfect government, and utilize perfect wisdom! This wisdom will be revealed once our fleshly limitations are stripped away. It will be the most robust spring cleaning we have ever experienced! The old will be thrown out and in will come the new! We will be changed from fleshly mortal to fleshly immortal. We will no longer experience death, fatigue, pain, sadness, or anxiety! Perfection will have truly taken up residence here on earth!

> The fear of the Lord is the beginning of knowledge: but fools despise wisdom and instruction. (Proverbs 1:7, KJV)

> For the wisdom of this world is foolishness with God. For it is written, He catches the wise in their own craftiness. (1 Corinthians 3:19, NKJV)

> Therefore, to him who knows to do good and does not do it, to him it is sin. (James 4:17, NKJV)

> Your word I have hidden in my heart, That I might not sin against You. Blessed are You, O Lord! Teach me Your statutes. (Psalm 119:11, NKJV)

> Study to shew thyself approved unto God, a workman that needeth not to be ashamed, rightly dividing the word of truth. (2 Timothy 2:15, KJV)

> Where there is no revelation, the people
> cast off restraint; But happy is he who
> keeps the law. (Proverbs 29:18, NKJV)

It is important to understand that wisdom cannot be exercised unless there is an underlying base of knowledge, and the foundation of knowledge can only be laid with truth. If information is false, it cannot constitute knowledge because knowing something that is false means you are knowledgeable of nothing. Believing a lie puts us in worse position than lacking the understanding of truth. Attempting to obtain knowledge without truth is similar to baking a cake with sawdust instead of flour. The wrong ingredients will never achieve a desired outcome!

When we were children, our parents taught us that a fib should be avoided. Truth was boiled down to whether or not we were telling a lie. As adults truth can be much more difficult to ascertain. Often there are so many perspectives that we are simply unable to decipher the truth. If you need an example, turn to the news media! At any moment in time, multiple organizations, which purportedly specialize in journalism, will cover the same event, but will communicate opposing narratives. Journalism is a profession, which should remain unbiased, but is currently far from professional. How can a profession, whose sole purpose is to deliver a true message, have so much trouble in finding truth? The problem lies in humanity.

As humans we are biased by what we think we know. Remember that knowledge is impossible without truth; therefore, if our knowledge is built on lies, we will consistently arrive at a wrong conclusion. Heads full of useless misinformation cause us to increasingly fill our heads with more useless misinformation. As humans we will often dismiss evidence that opposes our opinion if it appears to be an anomaly. If our head is full of misinformation, we will literally parse out truth in order to retain a lie. We are reluctant to discard a closely held value until the evidence is so overwhelming that it simply cannot be ignored. This is where Satan specializes in his attack strategy. Satan's favorite tactic is to overload our senses with mountains of misinformation; this is especially problematic since we are prone to discard anomalies. Humans are more likely to accept an idea if it is supported by a majority of their peers. This is why humans are quite literally incapable of producing an unbiased opinion; this flaw causes us to be innately blind when it comes to truth.

Truth blindness is a curse in our world today! Society has weaponized democracy by demonizing dissent. Democracy has been applied to every facet of society. The majority view is now touted as truth. Truth no longer matters as long as the largest populous supports the lie. The voice of the majority is used to drown out any opposing view; the opposition is ostracized through belittling speech, satire, and narrative control. These tactics have been employed to redefine sacred vows, normalize abominable behavior, hinder Godly conviction, and sear our collective conscience. It is no wonder the Bible warns of the power of an evil tongue (Psalm 140:1-3; James 3:6, KJV).

Another hindrance to truth is the partial truth. Something can be true, but not necessarily be the full truth. For instance, if a bully claims that a child attacked him, but in actuality it was his relentless taunting that provoked the punch to his nose; this information is vital to determining responsibility. It is true that the child attacked the bully, but the blame is mutually shared. You can see how context can change perception, which is what makes truth so difficult to determine. Unless we know all of the facts, we will likely be unable to recognize truth. This appears to place us in a quandary; it appears that we have to know everything in order to properly arrive at any truth. Obviously this is impossible because we are finite humans and rarely know all of the facts of any given situation. Remember, truth is critical to knowledge.

In lieu of relegating ourselves to a life of stupidity, we have another option! Truth is readily available to us! God knew that we would be unable to recognize truth on our own. This is why He gave us the Bible. According to God, doing what is right in our own eyes often means we do the wrong thing (Proverbs 12:15, KJV). It is possible to have good intentions while performing the wrong action. Have you ever lost a loved one and had someone tell you that they know exactly how you feel? It is especially offensive when there is an accompanying story to prove their claim. My sister passed away earlier this year, so I can personally attest to this particular scenario. I do not believe most people intentionally try to be offensive, but sometimes we just do not know how to succeed. It is part of being human. We do not have all of the facts; therefore, we fall back on our perception. Our perception causes us to render judgment with little to no fact. We quickly weigh the little information we have and make hasty decisions based on our feelings. This is why we must not make important decisions based on our perception. It is fine to pick a restaurant or shopping destination this way, but most of our lives should be carefully considered against a proper source of truth. It is only at the point where truth is found that knowledge can begin to be accumulated. When a bank of knowledge is compiled, and we have learned how to apply that knowledge to our lives, wisdom is achieved.

If truth is so important, how can we be certain that we are finding and utilizing truth in our search for knowledge? You should be happy to know that there is a source of truth, and it is possible to know truth's origin! Imagine for a moment that you designed a new invention. You wanted to market this new invention to the public, so you patented the design, hired a manufacturer, signed contracts with department stores, and began producing your product. Because you wanted to make sure people use your product in a manner that is consistent with your design, you included a manual in every box of product that is produced. It is your desire that customers understand and utilize your product in the correct manner.

This scenario perfectly describes God's creation. He designed all of creation with His own intent. God wants His creation to be used in the exact manner for which He created it. Humans have no right to repurpose God's invention! God cares a great deal about how His creation is utilized, so He created a manual to help guide our usage! God is the source of truth, and His Word is our manual that helps us find His truth!

If a man or woman knows something that is false, but thinks it to be true, this wisdom is foolishness. This type of foolish wisdom will be absolved once Christ begins to rule the world.

For this reason, we must begin our search for truth with the fear of the Lord. This means we start by seeking to understand God's principles. Why start anywhere other than the Engineer and Producer of the universe? God designed this world to function and work according to His specifications. The very concept of sin is when humans attempt to use God's creation in a manner in which He hates and for which it was not designed. Sin is not only performing an action that is specifically named in the Bible as displeasing to God. Sin is defined by James as failure to do that which is right. How will we know what is right unless we study God's Word? How will we know how God's creation should be used unless we read God's manual? This is why David said, "Your word I have hidden in my heart, That I might not sin against You...Teach me Your statutes" (Psalm 119:11, NKJV). David desired to know and memorize God's manual in order to ensure adherence to God's design! Paul instructed Timothy about the importance of "rightly dividing the word of truth" (2 Timothy 2:15, KJV). Paul was not talking about severing the Bible or obeying only a portion of God's Word; instead, he was stressing the criticality of properly interpreting and applying the Word of God! God's Word is the source of truth! If something you know conflicts with God's Word, it is meaningless misinformation because it is a lie. God's Word is always true because it is God's explanation concerning His creation; only God can explain His own intent! To have wisdom, we must first have knowledge, and, to have knowledge, we must study the Word of God in order to find truth! Solomon tells us that if people do not have proper revelation, they are unable to obey God (Proverbs 29:18, NKJV). However, those that know and obey God's law have true happiness! I would like to add that those people also have and exercise wisdom.

There is only one God, and His name is Jesus! Yahweh, the God of the Jews, is the same God of the Christians! The Spirit that resurrected Jesus Christ is that one true God; He holds all power in heaven and in earth! The human Jesus, the body of God and offspring of Mary, died in order to offer a blood sacrifice for atonement of our sins! Now that He has been transformed into His new body, Jesus Christ rules and reigns in heaven! God will continue to manifest, or make Himself visible, to all creation in His resurrected, transformed body, which is the body of Jesus Christ. According to John, the Lamb sits alone on the throne in heaven (Revelation 5:6, NKJV). Jesus is the face of God; He currently inhabits the throne of the one true and living God. Jesus Christ remains the only way, the only truth, and the only life for all mankind!

FIVE

The Victory of God

The Pathway

We know that God manifested and continues to manifest Himself in the body of Jesus Christ. In fact, God will return to earth a second time in the same human body that was resurrected approximately two thousand years ago! When Jesus appeared on earth the first time, He was here as a sacrifice for sin. However, when He reappears, it will be to: collect the people that are called by His name, battle the enemies of Israel, and win victory over Satan! God is using the manifestation of Christ for a precise reason. Remember that when God manifests Himself, it is for a specific purpose and period of time. Once the purpose is fulfilled, the manifestation will end, and it is always possible that God may choose to express Himself through a new manifestation.

Beware lest anyone cheat you through philosophy and empty deceit, according to the tradition of men, according to the basic principles of the world, and not according to Christ. For in Him dwells all the fullness of the Godhead bodily; and you are complete in Him, who is the head of all principality and power. (Colossians 2:8-10, NKJV)

But this He spoke concerning the Spirit, whom those believing in Him would receive; for the Holy Spirit was not yet given, because Jesus was not yet glorified. (John 7:39, NKJV)

Has in these last days spoken to us by His Son, whom He has appointed heir of all things, through whom also He made the worlds; who being the brightness of His glory and the express image of His person, and upholding all things by the word of His power, when He had by Himself purged our sins, sat down at the right hand of the Majesty on high. (Hebrews 1:2-3, NKJV)

And Jesus came and spoke to them, saying,
All authority has been given to Me in
heaven and on earth. (Matthew 28:18,
NKJV)

After Jesus' death, burial, and resurrection, He was glorified
and ascended into heaven. Glorified is not a common word in
our everyday vernacular. Sometimes we breeze over words
that are unfamiliar to us without taking the time to understand
their meaning. This word could be an easy candidate for this
treatment, but it is far too important to be handled in this
manner!

What does the Bible mean when it says Jesus was glorified?
As we mentioned earlier, glorify means to render glorious or to
make honorable (Strong, Doxazo Meaning in Bible - New
Testament Greek Lexicon - King James Version 1890). After
Jesus was resurrected, He was given honor and glory! This may
seem to be an insignificant detail, but it actually speaks
volumes! For a human person to receive glory and honor in
heaven is very significant! Here on earth we might honor a
local hero for bravery or throw a birthday party for someone
that reaches a milestone age, but to receive honor and glory in
heaven is a much more significant event! The awards in heaven
are only granted for lifetime achievement!

The glory and honor given to Jesus after His death was unlikely anything any human has ever experienced. The writer of Hebrews said God's "glory and...express image...sat down at the right hand of the Majesty on high" (Hebrews 1:2-3, NKJV). In the last chapter, we called attention to the fact that God does not have hands. Instead, this verse is informing us that Jesus Christ was given the glory of God! In ancient days, the right hand signified the source of power. Here it is identifying Jesus as the entity with the power, but not just some of the power; Jesus has all of God's power! Obviously this is another way of saying Jesus is God in flesh! Jesus humbled Himself in becoming a weak mortal man and then glorified Himself to hold all power in heaven and earth as the immortal, Almighty God!

Before Jesus ascended into heaven, He informed His disciples that He had been given "all authority...in heaven and...earth" (Matthew 28:18, NKJV). The Messiah took on all authority, all power, all honor, and the fullness of God; He became the head of the Spirit of God. Notice that Paul issues a warning and then follows that warning with the truth that should be protected and believed! He said, "Beware lest anyone cheat you through philosophy and empty deceit" (Colossians 2:8, NKJV). Paul then goes on to explain truth, which is the opposite of deceit; Paul tells us that Jesus is "the head of all principality and power" (Colossians 2:8-10, NKJV). In other words, deceit would tell you that Jesus is subordinate to or coequal with, but the truth is that Jesus is supreme! He is the principal holder of any and all power!

In this book we, have talked about Jesus as being one of many manifestations of God; God has used many throughout history. This is absolutely true; however, the Bible gives particular significance to the manifestation of Jesus Christ. We mentioned before that each manifestation is designed for a specific purpose. Just as the partial hand to Belshazzar was intentional, Jesus, the son of man, is also intentional!

> Thomas said to Him, Lord, we do not know
> where You are going, and how can we
> know the way? Jesus said to him, I am the
> way, the truth, and the life. No one comes
> to the Father except through Me. (John
> 14:5-6, NKJV)

> For I am not ashamed of the gospel of
> Christ, for it is the power of God to
> salvation for everyone who believes, for
> the Jew first and also for the Greek.
> (Romans 1:16, NKJV)

Thomas did not understand Jesus' teachings, so he asked Jesus, "We do not know where You are going, and how can we know the way?" (John 14:5-6, NKJV) In other words, Thomas was asking: How can we go where you are going? Jesus' response was clear: Mankind can only go where I go if he or she obeys the path I take. A path leads to a destination; paths are typically worn due to frequent use. With each new traveler, grass and foliage become increasingly trampled and the path becomes visibly worn. Jesus' death, burial, and resurrection are the path we must take in order to arrive at the same destination as Jesus. Over the years, this path has become increasingly obvious as many thousands of people have journeyed this course and arrived at their destination! God coined this path in the Bible as: salvation. The "gospel of Christ" is the "power of God to salvation" (Romans 1:16, NKJV). Salvation cannot be attained except through the gospel of Christ!

> He was oppressed and He was afflicted, Yet He opened not His mouth; He was led as a lamb to the slaughter, And as a sheep before its shearers is silent, So He opened not His mouth. (Isaiah 53:7, NKJV)

> The next day John saw Jesus coming
> toward him, and said, Behold! The Lamb of
> God who takes away the sin of the world!
> (John 1:29, NKJV)

One of our most challenging foes has been defeated by Jesus Christ; He has won the victory over sin! In chapter one, we alluded to Jesus as *the Lamb*. This designation was prophesied by Isaiah; he may or may not have realized the significance of his words, but he prophesied that Jesus would act as a lamb that was being sacrificed (Isaiah 53:7, NKJV). In many instances, animal sacrifices in ancient Israel were performed in order to atone for sin. Atone simply means to settle a debt owed for wrong action (Merriam-Webster, n.d.). However, these ancient sin sacrifices served only as a temporary atonement for sin because they were required annually. Every year Jews were required to feed, groom, transport, slaughter, and sacrifice animals at the Temple in Jerusalem. The debt of sin was never truly erased, but only postponed one year at a time; this process was repeated year after year. However, this all changed when Jesus stepped onto the scene!

John the Baptist spoke for all to hear, "Behold! The Lamb of God who takes away the sin of the world" (John 1:29, NKJV).

The perfect sacrificial Lamb would pay the ultimate price for the sins of all humanity! The blood of Jesus became the bartering token to settle the sin debt for all mankind! This ultimate, sacrificial payment became the victory over sin, which is the Gospel, or good news, of Jesus Christ! We all love hearing good news! The good news of Jesus Christ is that through this path we can obtain salvation! Not a salvation that must be repeated year after year, but a salvation that is forever! It pays in full the debt we owe for past sins, and it gives us the power we need to overcome sin each and every day thereafter.

Obviously we are not scourged with a cat of nine tails nor are we ridiculed, assaulted, or physically murdered on a cross! Instead, ours is a spiritual death, and it is absolutely required if we want to obtain salvation! A spiritual path does, however, require physical action!

> Moreover, brethren, I declare to you the gospel which I preached to you, which also you received and in which you stand, by which also you are saved, if you hold fast that word which I preached to you—unless you believed in vain. For I delivered to you first of all that which I also received: that Christ died for our sins according to the

Scriptures, and that He was buried, and
that He rose again the third day according
to the Scriptures. (1 Corinthians 15:1-4,
NKJV)

The gospel is a term that is discussed worldwide; people all
over the world talk about the gospel and many people
recognize the term. Even though people are familiar with the
term, most people cannot define it. People might attempt to
summarize it by claiming it is: the good news of Jesus Christ,
the sacrifice of Jesus, four of the books of the New Testament,
loving people like Christ loved us, or a myriad of other
explanations. However, regardless of various beliefs about the
gospel, Paul actually gives us the answer! Paul tells us that the
gospel by which we are saved is Christ's death, burial, and
resurrection (1 Corinthians 15:1-4, NKJV). This definition may
not resonate with you, and some may ask: What does that
even mean? Paul was drawing a correlation between the path
Jesus took through His physical death and the path that all of
us must take in our spiritual death! We will further discuss
each of these in subsequent paragraphs.

Repent therefore and be converted, that
your sins may be blotted out, so that times

of refreshing may come from the presence
of the Lord. (Acts 3:19, NKJV)

But declared first to those in Damascus and
in Jerusalem, and throughout all the region
of Judea, and then to the Gentiles, that
they should repent, turn to God, and do
works befitting repentance. (Acts 26:20,
NKJV)

First, there is the death. Just as physical death is permanent,
a spiritual death should be just as serious! Notice how Luke
informs us to: "Repent, turn to God, and do works befitting
repentance" (Acts 26:20, NKJV). Spiritual death requires a
decision, a confession, and continual action! Spiritual death
requires us to make a decision to stop displeasing God, it
requires us to verbally ask God to forgive us for past actions
that displeased Him, and it requires us to change our lifestyle!
True repentant, spiritual death requires a change that is not
temporary!

Therefore we were buried with Him
through baptism into death, that just as
Christ was raised from the dead by the

glory of the Father, even so we also should
walk in newness of life. (Romans 6:4, NKJV)

Jesus answered, Most assuredly, I say to
you, unless one is born of water and the
Spirit, he cannot enter the kingdom of God.
(John 3:5, NKJV)

Then Peter said to them, Repent, and let
every one of you be baptized in the name
of Jesus Christ for the remission of sins;
and you shall receive the gift of the Holy
Spirit. (Acts 2:38, NKJV)

Second, there is the burial. Paul described that we are
buried with Jesus through baptism (Romans 6:4, NKJV). Jesus
said there are two types of baptisms: a physical baptism and a
spiritual baptism (John 3:5, NKJV). Peter tells us that baptism in
water is for remission of sin (Acts 2:38, NKJV). After we
spiritually die through repentance, the dead man or woman
must be buried in water. During this water burial, Peter says
the name of Jesus must be invoked (Acts 2:38, NKJV). This is
important because this is how we tie Jesus' physical death to
our spiritual death! The physical blood that Jesus shed at
Calvary is the spiritual payment for our sins; Peter said it is "for

the remission of sins" (Acts 2:38, NKJV). If we go down into the water without the name, we are just getting wet; however, if the name accompanies the water burial, the payment transaction is complete! The debt we accrued through past sin is paid in full!

> And they were all filled with the Holy Spirit and began to speak with other tongues, as the Spirit gave them utterance. (Acts 2:4, NKJV)

> However, when He, the Spirit of truth, has come, He will guide you into all truth; for He will not speak on His own authority, but whatever He hears He will speak; and He will tell you things to come. (John 16:13, NKJV)

Third, there is the resurrection. Jesus talked about a second baptism, which is being born of the Spirit (John 3:5, NKJV). Peter called this second baptism a "gift of the Holy Spirit" (Acts 2:38, NKJV). Jesus experienced a resurrection where His physical body came back to life after death. While it is true that there will be a future event that many refer to as the Resurrection, which will take place when Christ returns to collect His people; right now we are only referencing a spiritual event that is presently available to everyone! We have been talking about following a spiritual path that parallels the literal path of Jesus. We can experience a spiritual resurrection during the course of our lives; this is when we rise to walk in newness of life! Our old life is dead and our new life in Christ begins! Spiritual death and burial are life changing decisions, but neither compare to spiritual resurrection! It is wonderful to make a decision to change and take action to procure payment for past sins! Spiritual death and burial takes care of the past, but there is also a future!

Jesus talked about a "Spirit of truth" that will "guide you into all truth" (John 16:13, NKJV). We require spiritual resurrection in order to have the Spirit of truth alive in our lives. Any person that veers from a path will fail to reach their desired destination. Spiritual resurrection is part of the path Jesus gave us to follow. Without the Holy Spirit, we will fail to find full truth and will be incapable of arriving at Jesus' destination! The Spirit of truth is the most important gift that any person will ever receive! Jesus told Nicodemus that it is a requirement for entering into the Kingdom of God! Without the Holy Spirit, we will be excluded from the Kingdom of God. Luke documented that we will know when we are spiritually resurrected because we will be filled with the Holy Spirit, or

Spirit of truth, and will speak with "other tongues" (Acts 2:4, NKJV). No one accidentally or unknowingly receives the Spirit of God, and there is no reason to doubt because God gives us definitive proof when He takes up residence!

> And to give you who are troubled rest with us when the Lord Jesus is revealed from heaven with His mighty angels, in flaming fire taking vengeance on those who do not know God, and on those who do not obey the gospel of our Lord Jesus Christ. These shall be punished with everlasting destruction from the presence of the Lord and from the glory of His power. (2 Thessalonians 1:7-9, NKJV)

Reverend Irvin Baxter explains that there will be a negative result for those who do not obey the gospel of Jesus Christ (Baxter, 2015). There will be a very undesirable fate for those who do not follow Jesus' death, burial, and resurrection in their own lives. It is absolutely paramount that we choose to spiritually die in repentance, be buried in water in the name of Jesus, and rise to walk in newness of life by being filled with the Spirit of truth. We can be certain that the Holy Spirit has been received because it will be accompanied by the proof of audible speech in an unknown language!

Jesus' death, burial, and resurrection are the spiritual path we must take to salvation! God chose to reveal His name through the human Messiah. That Messiah continues to be the primary interaction point for all of us today. Invoking the name of Jesus is critical because power is in that name. Healing, deliverance, miracles, and salvation are all available through the name of Jesus! It is a name that is higher than any other name!

We know that God can do anything He wants; however, there are two apparent reasons for God to choose to manifest Himself in a human body. First, He is doing it for our benefit. It is for our benefit that He took on the form of a human body and became the perfect, sinless sacrifice for our sins. This made Him the perfect example by which we should pattern our lives. Additionally, a physical form gave people a material being that can be seen, heard, and touched; this will once again be true when He returns to earth a second time. He will establish a kingdom here on earth and rule as our King in human form. He will rule the earth in perfect peace and harmony! We will be able to worship Him, communicate with Him, and co-rule alongside Him. Secondly, God chooses to represent Himself through a physical body because He loves mankind, and it is part of His plan to redeem us. After the fall of mankind in the garden, God promised that a human man would defeat Satan and God cannot lie. The defeat of Satan will break the curse of sin, and it will release humans to live an *enemy free* life throughout eternity with the One who first loved us!

From Innocence to Imperfection

> Therefore, just as through one man sin entered the world, and death through sin, and thus death spread to all men, because all sinned. (Romans 5:12, NKJV)

> But if the Spirit of Him who raised Jesus from the dead dwells in you, He who raised Christ from the dead will also give life to your mortal bodies through His Spirit who dwells in you. (Romans 8:11, NKJV)

> Behold, I was brought forth in iniquity, And in sin my mother conceived me. (Psalm 51:5, NKJV)

It was through Adam and Eve that sin entered into the world. From Adam until now, all of mankind has been born with a propensity, or an innate desire, to sin. When Eve took a bite of the forbidden fruit, her eyes were enlightened; she was never again able to close the door that she opened. The first time a child sins, it is similar to Eve's initial bite, and each subsequent sin is another bite of that forbidden fruit. This is how innocence is eroded by evil, but there is no remedy to return evil back to innocence. Christ has the ability to forgive our sins, but those sins leave a lasting impression upon us. When we sin, we gain first-hand knowledge of that which we previously did not know. Sin brings shame because God wants us to be aware of our mistakes, and, without awareness, we would be powerless to seek remediation. Since it is impossible to reverse the effects of experience, we must turn to Christ in order to help us cover our sins. In lieu of turning back time in order to return to a former state of healthy innocence, God helps us cover our evil memories. The Holy Spirit prompts us to set boundaries in areas that would otherwise leave us exposed and susceptible to sin. He helps us feed our mind with productive thoughts in order to drown out past sinful experiences, which results in personal convictions that help us avoid potentially dangerous snares. It also helps protect us from the memory of our past. If we put a personal boundary in front of our stumbling block, we will not experience the pain and injury associated with a fall.

Innocence is the state in which every human is born into this world. Even though men and women are born with an inclination to sin, people remain sinless until they actually plan or perform a sinful act. Notice Paul says, "Death spread to all men, because all sinned" (Romans 5:12, NKJV). In this passage, Paul is explaining that, if given enough time, humans are destined to fail because, due to the sinful nature, our flesh is weak. When David said, "In sin my mother conceived me", he was admitting his weakness and need of help (Psalm 51:4, NKJV). David was not saying that he committed sin while in his mother's womb nor did he somehow inherit sins that were committed prior to his birth. David was simply linking his adultery with Bathsheba and murder of Uriah to his inherited sinful nature; a nature that loved to sin and oppose God. David was making it known that, without God, it was impossible for him to avoid sin because his human nature was ungodly! Jesus is our perfect example because, just like all of us, He was born sinless; however, unlike any of us, He abstained from sin and never once gave in to temptation. This was only possible because Jesus was filled with the Holy Spirit from conception, which gives us hope! This is our hope: Once we are filled with the same Spirit that raised Christ from the dead, we too have an opportunity to overcome sin and live a life free from sin.

The Victor

Therefore My Father loves Me, because I
lay down My life that I may take it again.
(John 10:17, NKJV)

He went a little farther and fell on His face,
and prayed, saying, O My Father, if it is
possible, let this cup pass from Me;
nevertheless, not as I will, but as You will.
(Matthew 26:39, NKJV)

Then Jesus answered and said to them,
Most assuredly, I say to you, the Son can
do nothing of Himself, but what He sees
the Father do; for whatever He does, the
Son also does in like manner. For the
Father loves the Son, and shows Him all
things that He Himself does; and He will
show Him greater works than these, that
you may marvel. (John 5:19-20, NKJV)

For we do not have a High Priest who
cannot sympathize with our weaknesses,
but was in all points tempted as we are,
yet without sin. (Hebrews 4:15, NKJV)

To him who overcomes I will grant to sit
with Me on My throne, as I also overcame
and sat down with My Father on His
throne. (Revelation 3:21, NKJV)

Jesus was born with free will to do as He pleased; He was
not forced to obey the Spirit of God. In fact, just as any other
human, He could have fallen prey to fleshly lusts at any
moment during His lifetime. Sin was waiting around every
corner for the duration of Jesus' existence as a mortal man.
The flesh of Jesus desired sin, and His carnality made Him as
weak as any other human; however, the Spirit that resided in
His body was the Holy Spirit of Almighty God! We know that
Jesus was born with a sinful nature because He was tempted in
every respect. The desire to sin is a result of our fallen sinful
nature; therefore, it is an intrinsic part of humanity. Since the
Garden of Eden, it has simply become a part of the human
experience. We know that Jesus was fully Human because He
needed food and water to survive, developed relationships and
felt emotion, experienced pain and suffering, wanted to rebel
against His conscience, and was tempted to commit sinful acts.
However, Jesus was successful where we all have failed. We
have failed because none of us have successfully avoided sin.

We are all guilty of committing sinful acts throughout our lives. However, Jesus overcame His fleshly desires and refused to surrender His integrity; He refrained from enjoying the temporary pleasures of sin! In His flesh, Jesus did not have an advantage over us, which was by design. His purpose was to humble Himself by putting Himself in the exact position in which every human finds himself or herself. For Jesus to take our place on the cross and pay the penalty for our sin, He had to start from the same position from which we all began. Jesus said, "To him who overcomes...as I also overcame" (Revelation 3:21, NKJV). How did Jesus overcome? He overcame by sacrificing His flesh and surrendering to the Spirit that taught Him. How should we overcome? We overcome the same way Jesus overcame; through obedience to the Holy Spirit! The flesh of Jesus did not offer Him an advantage, but the Spirit of Jesus gave Him power! All humans have this same opportunity! The secret weapon of Jesus, which allowed Him to live a sinless life, is available to all of us! We have the opportunity to be filled with the Spirit of God!

It is important to remember that the flesh of Jesus was exactly like ours! If we were not on a level playing field, we would be forced to overcome more than Jesus overcame! If Jesus had an easier road that all of us, He would not be our perfect example! If Jesus had an advantage, His sacrifice would be cheapened and less significant. However, we know this is not true! His sacrifice was not cheap; Christ walked the road of humanity and He finished as the victor! Jesus took what appeared to be an impossible task, and He made it possible for every one of us! He walked a mile in our shoes so to speak, and proved to us that we can achieve the same results that He achieved!

Jesus submitted to the guidance of the Holy Spirit and refused to follow after His fleshly desires. This is exactly how you and I should live our lives. If we follow the example set by Jesus, we will avoid the negative ramifications of disobedience, and we will gain the rewards of obedience. The human Jesus obeyed the Spirit that dwelt inside of Him; if we are filled with the same Spirit of God and obey His Spirit, our destination will be the same as His destination! Those who obey spiritual resurrection will also take part in a physical resurrection! After Jesus Christ returns to earth to collect His saints, we will accompany Him wherever He goes throughout eternity!

Christ Returns

> For you yourselves know perfectly that the
> day of the Lord so comes as a thief in the
> night. For when they say, Peace and safety!
> then sudden destruction comes upon

them, as labor pains upon a pregnant woman. And they shall not escape. But you, brethren, are not in darkness, so that this Day should overtake you as a thief. You are all sons of light and sons of the day. We are not of the night nor of darkness. Therefore let us not sleep, as others do, but let us watch and be sober. (1 Thessalonians 5:2-6, NKJV)

For this we say to you by the word of the Lord, that we who are alive and remain until the coming of the Lord will by no means precede those who are asleep. For the Lord Himself will descend from heaven with a shout, with the voice of an archangel, and with the trumpet of God. And the dead in Christ will rise first. Then we who are alive and remain shall be caught up together with them in the clouds to meet the Lord in the air. And thus we shall always be with the Lord. (1 Thessalonians 4:15-17, NKJV)

So the seven angels who had the seven
trumpets prepared themselves to sound.
(Revelation 8:6, NKJV)

Then the seventh angel sounded: And
there were loud voices in heaven, saying,
The kingdoms of this world have become
the kingdoms of our Lord and of His Christ,
and He shall reign forever and ever!
(Revelation 11:15, NKJV)

Leading up to Jesus' physical return to earth, there are
seven events that are prophesied to occur; the last of which
will be Christ's actual descent back down to earth from heaven
(Endtime Blog, Revelation: The Seven Trumpets and When
They Shall Sound 2014). The Bible refers to these seven events
as "trumpets", and the occurrence of each event is likened to
the sounding of a trumpet (Revelation 8:6, NKJV). The sounding
of each trumpet, or the occurrence of each event, is designed
to provide evidence that the return of Jesus is swiftly
approaching. In addition to these seven trumpets, there are
many other prophecies that will help us identify Christ's return.
Most people that live through these events will be completely
unaware of their importance! However, there will be some
that will recognize these events as precursors, or distinguishing

signs, leading up to His return! The Bible cautions us to be aware of the second coming of Christ by watching for Biblical prophecies as they transpire. If we do not anticipate His coming by watching for His signs, we will be caught unaware. It is absolutely critical that we are prepared to meet Christ when He returns!

Christ's return to earth will be quite different than His first coming! His second coming will be heralded by an angel; this angelic proclamation is the seventh and final trumpet (1 Thessalonians 4:15-17, NKJV). In this passage, Paul identifies two classes of people during the years leading up to Christ's return. The first group consists of people of darkness, and the second group is the people of light. Paul says that the people of darkness are asleep, and the people of light are awake and watchful!

We are able to see that Paul uses metaphors for multiple purposes. The variance between light and darkness is a common theme in the Bible. Light is often used to describe Godliness and righteousness; darkness frequently describes evil and sin. Paul also uses light and darkness to contrast people that are paying attention against those that are apathetic. Additionally, people of light are those that understand prophetic significance, but people of darkness do not comprehend. The Holy Spirit is the light that enables us to see by revealing the Word of God to us and by convicting our hearts. Without the Holy Spirit in our lives, we stumble through this life as if immersed in thick darkness. Based on what we have discussed, there are two ways people can be blinded by darkness: through hatred of God or by lack of effort. Passivity in our spiritual walk places us in the same category as those that willingly choose to oppose God.

People are only able to see light when they are conscious; therefore, Paul describes our state of spiritual awareness as either being awake or asleep. If we are knowledgeable about God's Word, which includes His prophecies, then we are awake; if we are ignorant about God then we are asleep. As humans, we see a huge gray area between people that are trying versus those that are not. We would like to make three, four, or maybe even more categories of people; however, the Bible consistently draws a single line between two categories. The line is drawn between those that are in light versus those that are in darkness. We are either following God or we are walking away from Him.

Since thirty percent of the Bible is prophetic in nature, we would have to apply great effort in order to avoid prophecy while reading God's Word (Robbins, 2020). In fact, all of God's Word should be consumed in our pursuit of spiritual alertness! I have heard people comment that they avoid the book of

Revelation because it is difficult to understand. I have also heard people say that they are not concerned with prophecy as long as their heart is ready to meet Christ. We cannot say that seventy percent of the Bible is beneficial while discounting thirty percent. The whole Bible is either beneficial or it is not; however, we know that the whole Bible is beneficial! Every single word is the Word of God! While not everyone will enjoy Biblical prophecy, the whole Bible is for everyone. Treating the Bible like a buffet is an unwise approach to reading scripture. "All scripture...is profitable" (2 Timothy 3:16, KJV). This is why we must consume every last Word!

Paul tells us that people of darkness will not be aware of Christ's return, and they will be so blinded by darkness that His return will be as startling as a thief that surprises them during the night (1 Thessalonians 5:2, NKJV). The reason for this surprise is because people of darkness will not recognize the preliminary signs found in God's Word! The children of light will be anticipating Christ's return, preparing to meet Him, and watching for the signs of His coming! If we do not sleep, we will be able to decipher the signs and know when Christ will return! Paul assures us that Christ's return will not catch His people like a thief catches unsuspecting victims (1 Thessalonians 5:2-5, NKJV). However, those that are asleep will be caught unaware (Matthew 24:43-44, KJV). Paul says children of the light should "not sleep, as others do, but...watch and be sober" (1 Thessalonians 5:6, NKJV). How do we watch, stay awake, and remain sober? We study the Word of God, pray for revelation, and seek guidance from those who have been endowed with a gift of prophecy. At the end of this chapter, we will discuss the gift of prophecy in greater detail. Paul conveys to us that, as the seventh trumpet is sounding, Jesus will descend from heaven, His saints will ascend from earth, and we all will meet while suspended in the air (1 Thessalonians 4:16-17, NKJV).

> Now, brethren, concerning the coming of our Lord Jesus Christ and our gathering together to Him, we ask you, not to be soon shaken in mind or troubled, either by spirit or by word or by letter, as if from us, as though the day of Christ had come. Let no one deceive you by any means; for that Day will not come unless the falling away comes first, and the man of sin is revealed, the son of perdition, who opposes and exalts himself above all that is called God or that is worshiped, so that he sits as God in the temple of God, showing himself that he is God. (2 Thessalonians 2:1-4, NKJV)

So they worshiped the dragon who gave authority to the beast; and they worshiped the beast, saying, Who is like the beast? Who is able to make war with him? And he was given a mouth speaking great things and blasphemies, and he was given authority to continue for forty-two months. (Revelation 13:4-5, NKJV)

Then he shall confirm a covenant with many for one week; But in the middle of the week He shall bring an end to sacrifice and offering. And on the wing of abominations shall be one who makes desolate, Even until the consummation, which is determined, Is poured out on the desolate. (Daniel 9:27, NKJV)

But he who endures to the end shall be saved. And this gospel of the kingdom will be preached in all the world as a witness to all the nations, and then the end will come. Therefore when you see the abomination of desolation, spoken of by Daniel the prophet, standing in the holy place

(whoever reads, let him understand).
(Matthew 24:13-15, NKJV)

While Paul was alive there was a false belief that the return of Jesus Christ was imminent, which means people believed that He was about to return at any moment; however, Paul soundly disagreed with this theory. Paul told the people of his day, "We ask you, not to be...troubled...as though the day of Christ had come" (2 Thessalonians 2:1-2, NKJV). In this verse, "had come" is translated to English from a Greek word that means: near or close at hand (Strong, Enistemi Meaning in Bible - New Testament Greek Lexicon - King James Version 1890). Paul told these people, which were anticipating Christ's return at any moment, that their expectation was unfounded. Paul went on to say, "Let no one deceive you by any means; for that Day will not come unless"; following this "unless" is a specific event that must occur before Jesus will return to earth (2 Thessalonians 2:3, NKJV). The resoundingly pivotal phrase in this verse is when Paul says, "That Day will not come unless"! The criterion that Paul laid out was this: Neither the second coming of Jesus nor the gathering of His saints will occur until after the revealing of a man he called "the son of perdition" (2 Thessalonians 2:1-4, NKJV).

The son of perdition is called by other names throughout the Bible. Daniel called him "the prince of the covenant" (Daniel 11:21-22, KJV). John referred to this man as the mouth of the beast (Revelation 13:4-5, NKJV). He also consolidated this phrase when he called him "the Beast" (Revelation 19:19, NKJV). Since this shorter title is more commonly recognized, we will use this term throughout the remainder of this book. John says that power was given unto this man to rule forty-two months, which totals up to three and one-half years (Revelation 13:5, NKJV). Daniel also prophesied about this duration of time when he said, "in the middle of the week" (Daniel 9:27, NKJV). In order to understand how half of a week equates to years of time, we must understand that Daniel is referring to "week" as a period of seven years, not days (Daniel 9:2, KJV). Daniel calls our attention to the fact that this week of years will be divided into two equal halves. Three very significant events will occur during this seven year period! It will begin with a peace treaty, the midway point will be marked by the Beast's rise to power, and the end will be crowned with the return of Jesus Christ!

First, there is the peace treaty that marks the beginning of this week of years. Daniel said the Beast "shall confirm a covenant with many for one week" (Daniel 9:27, NKJV). A covenant differs from a promise because it requires terms and conditions. God has made many covenants with people throughout history, but only three recorded in the Bible are still unfulfilled. Noah built an ark, and, as a result, God promised to never again destroy the earth by flood (Genesis 6:18; 9:11, KJV). This promise still applies to every person alive on earth! As we saw in chapter two, Abraham maintained a relationship with God, and, in return, God deeded land to his descendants forever. Abraham's living relatives still enjoy this promise today! As we saw earlier in this chapter, God also established a similar covenant with all mankind; if we obey the Gospel of Jesus Christ then we will inherit eternal life. This opportunity is still available to everyone that wishes to take advantage of it! Multiple covenants raise a legitimate question: If God has established multiple covenants, how do we know which covenant will be confirmed by the Beast? In order to answer this question, we must ascertain the people to which Daniel's prophecy is directed, and we must identify the covenant with the highest degree of relevancy to these people.

There are a couple of clues that identify the people to which this prophecy is given. This is an Old Testament prophecy given to Daniel, which is not absolute proof, but provides a hint that God is likely talking to the Jews. The more significant clue is when the prophecy discusses animal sacrifice (Daniel 9:27, NKJV). With exception of Jewish proselytes and people that assimilated into Jewish society, animal sacrifice has never been a part of gentile worship of Almighty God. This ceremony was commanded by God and practiced by the Jewish people. These two clues tell us with certainty that God is specifically addressing the nation of Israel in this prophecy.

Now we turn our attention to the benefits associated with each covenant; this will help us identify relevancy. The question we must answer is this: Why would the Beast confirm any of these ancient covenants? We must decide if the Beast's confirmation involves water destroying the earth, Israel's right to possess land located in the Middle East, or men and women living in eternity with Christ? In the current political climate, which has existed for over a century, the most likely candidate is Israel's right to inhabit the land. The land is central to all conflict between the Israeli and Palestinian peoples, which makes it a prime candidate for a peace treaty! We know that the confirmation is actually a treaty because it lasts for seven years, and its terms will be violated by the Beast.

This position is also supported in the fact that the promise to Abraham is closely related to the Jewish people. Noah's covenant is applicable to all of earth's inhabitants, and an eternal life with Christ is promised to all people that meet the criteria associated with being a saint of God. It is only Abraham's covenant that is predicated upon Jewish ancestry.

Based on this analysis, we can easily infer that the Beast will confirm God's promise involving the land of Israel.

As part of this seven year peace treaty, the Beast will confirm Israel's right to exist in the land that God promised to Abraham and his descendants. Daniel said, "He shall confirm a covenant with many for one week; But in the middle of the week He shall bring an end to sacrifices and offering" (Daniel 9:27, NKJV). It is important to understand that the conjunction "but" links animal sacrifices to this agreement (Daniel 9:27, NKJV). In this passage, the agreement will enable Israel to begin offering sacrifices, *but* this term of the agreement will be violated by the Beast. This also indicates the confirmation will concern a land treaty because Israel believes they are required by law to offer sacrifice to God on Mount Moriah, which requires a Jewish Temple in order to facilitate these ceremonies (Brinegar; Robbins, 2017). Mount Moriah is currently located within Israeli controlled territory, but is managed by a Jordanian Islamic group known as the Waqf (Baxter, 2015). Due to decades of Muslim and Jewish tension, a peace treaty is the necessary catalyst to allow the return of Jewish worship to Mount Moriah!

It appears that this peace agreement is just around the corner! As of this writing, Israel has normalized diplomatic relations with five Islamic neighbors: Egypt, Jordan, the United

Arab Emirates, Bahrain, and Sudan. Rumors suggest that several other nations in the region will be added to this list very soon! Regional support for Israel is paramount because this community of nations has been the backbone of Palestinian financial and political success for decades. However, pressure is mounting against the Palestinians to agree to terms of peace with Israel. Daniel prophesied over twenty-five hundred years ago that a peace agreement between Israel and the Palestinians will set the stage for the final seven years leading up to Christ's return! None of this was possible until the rebirth of the nation of Israel in 1948; since that time, all of the puzzle pieces have been coming together!

People may ask: How will we recognize the agreement prophesied by Daniel? We can identify Daniel's treaty by the Biblical requirements! The Bible gives five proofs that can be used to verify Daniels prophesied peace treaty (Baxter, 2020). According to Reverend Irvin Baxter, the peace agreement will: cause Israel to relinquish control of an area of land known as the West Bank, allow Jews to continue living in parts of the West Bank, allow Israel to retain control over the city of Jerusalem, place Mount Moriah under a multi-religion sharing arrangement, and open the way for Israel to build a Third Temple on Mount Moriah (Matthew 24:15-16, 21; Zechariah 14:2; Revelation 11:1-2, NKJV). If each requirement is fulfilled then we can easily recognize Daniel's prophesied treaty, which will act as a beacon signifying the beginning of the final seven years leading up to Christ's return!

Before we discuss the Beast's rise to power, we must first lay the groundwork to the government that he will rule. Just before Christ returns to earth, there will be one government that is vastly superior to all others that are in existence at that time. It will be a coalition of many nations that band together to form one massive entity. One instance of this prophecy was given by Daniel when he interpreted a dream for the king of Babylon (Daniel 2:31-47, KJV). In this dream, Nebuchadnezzar saw a statue that was constructed of various metals and clay; it had a head made of gold, chest and arms of silver, belly and thighs of brass, legs of iron, and feet of iron mixed with clay. Daniel told the king that the head of gold represented the kingdom of Babylon, and, following the Babylonian kingdom, five additional dominant kingdoms would rise to power.

In Nebuchadnezzar's dream, a rock superseded the final kingdom by crushing it; Daniel informs us that this rock is the God of heaven and the kingdom He establishes will never be destroyed (Daniel 2:34-44, KJV). The silver part of the statue represents the kingdom of the Medes and Persians, which overthrew the Babylonian empire in 539 B.C. (Baxter, 2015). This empire was then defeated by Alexander the Great, so the brass in the statue represents the Grecian Empire (Baxter, 2015). Following the Grecians were the Romans in 197 B.C.; this kingdom is represented by the legs of iron (Baxter, 2015). The Roman Empire was defeated in 476 A.D., and the next globally dominate empire to rise was the Holy Roman Empire in 800 A.D (Baxter, 2015). This empire consisted of the political Roman iron mixed with the religious Catholic clay (Baxter, 2015). This is the last empire outlined in Nebuchadnezzar's dream; therefore, it is this Holy Roman Empire that will be defeated by Christ at His return!

At this point, you may be asking yourself: How can Christ defeat a kingdom that was already defeated? This is an excellent question since Napoleon defeated the Holy Roman Empire in 1806; however, you should know that the Holy Roman Empire is rising once again (Baxter, 2012). The Bible foretells of a partnership between the Beast and a false prophet during the time of the iron and clay kingdom, which has always been the leadership structure of the Holy Roman Empire (Baxter, 2012). A king from Europe, accompanied by the Roman Catholic Pope, has always ruled the Holy Roman Empire. On November 19 of 2009, the first President of the European Union was elected, which set the stage for the Beast to rise to power (Baxter, 2012). It is also important to understand that the Roman Catholic Church has never ceased to exist, even after the fall of the Holy Roman Empire. Everything is in place for the Beast and false prophet to step onto the stage of world power!

This brings us back to the second major event that will take place during Daniel's final week of years. The exact midway point of the treaty will be marked by the Beast's rise to power. We have already discussed that the European Union will be the launching pad that catapults the Beast into power. Daniel informs us that the Beast will have the authority to restrict Jewish worship in the Temple; therefore, the Beast will be able to exercise control outside of Europe (Daniel 9:27, NKJV). The Beast will be the head of the European Union, which will wield massive authority in the United Nations; this is how the Beast will come to rule the world. At first it may appear to be a coalition, but eventually his rule will become a dictatorship. This leads us to an event where the Beast will foolishly attempt to seize control from God! After the Beast comes to power in the global government, he will travel to Israel, walk into the Jewish Temple, and inform the Jews that he is their long awaited messiah (2 Thessalonians 2:4, NKJV). As the self-proclaimed messiah, the Beast will ban animal sacrifices on Mount Moriah (Daniel 9:27, NKJV). After all, why would anyone offer animal sacrifices to a God that is standing right in front of them?

Impersonating God is a serious offense! It is not surprising that this event is given an ominous name, which was discussed by both Daniel and Jesus. Jesus provides direct correlation between the event He calls the "Abomination of Desolation" and the prophecies of Daniel (Matthew 24:15, NKJV). In this verse, Christ effectively confirmed that Daniel's week of years is synonymous with the period of time leading up to His return to earth! John says this man will have power for forty-two months, which, as we discussed, is the same amount of time prophesied by Daniel (Revelation 13:4-5, NKJV). The Beast will take global power at approximately the same time as this abominable event. He will likely be in the process of rising to power for many years prior to the Abomination of Desolation, which is evident since the Bible tells us that he will have previously participated in the Israeli peace treaty (Daniel 9:27, NKJV). However, he will violate terms of this agreement when he stops Israel from offering animal sacrifices in their Third Jewish Temple.

This may appear to occur out of sequence, but the peace treaty at the beginning of the final seven years will give Israel authority to inhabit at least a portion of the West Bank. We are discussing it now because it offers a good segue into the third significant event that occurs in Daniel's final week of years. Jesus prophesied that Israel would give away the West Bank

189

except for small indefensible portions of this land; He warned the Jews to flea this area after the treaty is violated at the Abomination of Desolation (Baxter, 2015). Jesus goes on to say that these indefensible segments of land will be invaded by the enemies of Israel after half of the seven year period has transpired; tragically, the Jews living in this area will be slaughtered (Matthew 24:17-21, NKJV). While under Israeli control, settlements were built throughout the West Bank; all along, the international community has strongly opposed these settlements (Baxter, 2015). Hundreds of thousands of Israelis live in these settlements and will temporarily be allowed to remain after the peace treaty is signed; however, this hope of peace will prove to be false (Baxter, 2015). The enemies of Israel will ultimately attack, abuse, rob, and murder these defenseless people.

Another area that is hotly contested prior to the peace treaty is Mount Moriah; the opposition has been so intense over this plot of ground that the Jews have been unable to erect a temple to facilitate their worship. This is why international agreement is so critical in opening the door to allow construction of this structure. The Beast's signature will be on this treaty, which allows temple worship, but the Bible prophesies that he will violate the agreement. The Abomination of Desolation occurs exactly in the middle of

Daniel's week of years, which tells us that the Beast's administration will last for the remaining three and one-half years.

The final event that occurs in this seven year period is the return of Christ to this earth! As we have previously discussed, the seventh trumpet occurs after the Great Tribulation. Keep in mind that the Beast is the catalyst for this tribulation, so it makes sense that this tumultuous time occurs during his reign over the world. Christ will return to remove the Beast from power and bring the Great Tribulation to a close!

Later in this chapter, we will discuss the implications of Christ's return in greater detail; therefore, we will take this opportunity to summarize the final seven years. Some significant events that have been prophesied to occur during this window of time are as follows: the Beast's participation in a seven year treaty that acknowledges Israel's right to exist in their ancestral homeland, the Beast comes to power at the exact midway point of this treaty, and Christ returns at the end of this treaty, which brings the Great Tribulation to a close.

The return of Jesus Christ is not imminent; there is a God ordained timeclock that is winding down, and there are specific milestones that are visibly transpiring in front of our eyes. Just as Paul explained, the Beast has to be revealed at the Abomination of Desolation before Christ will return to earth to collect His people! This grand, or not so grand, revealing of the Beast will happen in Jerusalem on Mount Moriah. Mount Moriah is also known as the Temple Mount because the first two Jewish temples were built on this mountain, and it will be the location of Israel's Third Temple (Brinegar & Robbins, 2017). The Beast's rise to power will usher in one of the worst periods in the history of mankind, but Christ will quickly return to defeat His foe and clean up the mess that has been accruing for over six thousand years!

> Then let those who are in Judea flee to the mountains. Let him who is on the housetop not go down to take anything out of his house. And let him who is in the field not go back to get his clothes. But woe to those who are pregnant and to those who are nursing babies in those days! And pray that your flight may not be in winter or on the Sabbath. For then there will be great tribulation, such as has not been since the beginning of the world until this time, no, nor ever shall be. (Matthew 24:16-21, NKJV)

Immediately after the tribulation of those days the sun will be darkened, and the moon will not give its light; the stars will fall from heaven, and the powers of the heavens will be shaken. Then the sign of the Son of Man will appear in heaven, and then all the tribes of the earth will mourn, and they will see the Son of Man coming on the clouds of heaven with power and great glory. And He will send His angels with a great sound of a trumpet, and they will gather together His elect from the four winds, from one end of heaven to the other. (Matthew 24:29-31, NKJV)

And then He will send His angels, and gather together His elect from the four winds, from the farthest part of earth to the farthest part of heaven. (Mark 13:27, NKJV)

And I saw the beast, the kings of the earth, and their armies, gathered together to make war against Him who sat on the horse and against His army. (Revelation 19:19, NKJV)

The Beast will come to power when he is revealed in Jerusalem at the Abomination of Desolation. It appears the Beast will take control over most of the world at this time and will rule mercilessly. We know that the Beast will rule mercilessly because, as soon as he begins to rule, the Bible foretells of a great tribulation that will last for the duration of his administration. We have already discussed that the Beast's administration will last for three and one-half years, and the reason his rule is so brief is due to the return of Jesus Christ! The Beast will only be allowed to rule for a very short time before an angel sounds the seventh trumpet announcing the return of Jesus Christ. Matthew recorded that Jesus will return "immediately after the tribulation" (Matthew 24:29-31, NKJV). Mark recorded that as Jesus returns He will "gather together His elect" from "the farthest part of earth" (Mark 13:27, NKJV). I hope the events are becoming very clear!

Paul says we will meet Jesus in the air after the seventh trumpet sounds; Matthew and Mark record that Jesus will return after the tribulation. Christ is giving everyone ample opportunity to wake up and take notice of His return! He has absolutely no desire to catch anyone off guard! He is not a God that is pulling the wool over anyone's eyes; He wants every person to know Him and prepare their hearts for His coming! It is true that many people will ignore the signs of His coming and will be caught off guard; however, that is not His will! His will is for everyone to find eternal life with Him (2 Peter 3:9, KJV). The scripture is clear that Christ will gather His people on His way back to earth as the seventh trumpet is sounding!

But leave out the court which is outside the temple, and do not measure it, for it has been given to the Gentiles. And they will tread the holy city underfoot for forty-two months. And I will give power to my two witnesses, and they will prophesy one thousand two hundred and sixty days, clothed in sackcloth. (Revelation 11:2-3, NKJV)

Although I heard, I did not understand. Then I said, My lord, what shall be the end of these things? And he said, Go your way, Daniel, for the words are closed up and sealed till the time of the end. Many shall be purified, made white, and refined, but the wicked shall do wickedly; and none of the wicked shall understand, but the wise shall understand. (Daniel 12:8-10, NKJV)

And out of one of them came a little horn which grew exceedingly great toward the south, toward the east, and toward the Glorious Land. And it grew up to the host of heaven; and it cast down some of the host and some of the stars to the ground, and trampled them. He even exalted himself as high as the Prince of the host; and by him the daily sacrifices were taken away, and the place of His sanctuary was cast down. (Daniel 8:9-11, NKJV)

Earlier we saw that Daniel prophesied a man, the same guy we have been referring to as *the Beast*, will stand in the Third Jewish Temple, and he will order the Jews to cease from offering animal sacrifices (Daniel 9:27, NKJV). John the revelator prophesied that, after this event, the world community will patrol the Temple Mount for forty-two months. Since the Beast will be the supreme leader of a global government, the gentile patrol will likely be a coalition of forces from the global community that are under his command. This coalition of global forces could possibly be initiated in order to ensure the Jews do not resume animal sacrifices on the Temple Mount. This is probable since, during the Beast's big reveal party, he will have just decreed an end to sacrifices. Going by Jewish history, it is very likely that some Jews will defy him and attempt to reinstate the sacrifices. Nonetheless, the sacrifices will be stopped, and the global dominance of the Beast will become incredibly strong; Daniel says the Beast "grew exceedingly great" (Daniel 8:9, NKJV).

There have been many large empires throughout history. However, the Beast's kingdom will be larger than any prior kingdom; it will stretch around the globe and engulf almost every nation on earth! However, it will not be even slightly comparable to the final Kingdom on earth! The final Kingdom is the sixth kingdom in Nebuchadnezzar's dream; the rock that demolishes the feet of the statue will become the Kingdom of God! Every person on earth will be subject to Christ's rule! During the vast majority of His final Kingdom on earth, there will be no war, no uprising, and no need to maintain a military (Isaiah 2:4, KJV). Satan will be bound at the beginning of Christ's Kingdom; however, the Bible foretells of a time during Christ's Millennial Kingdom that Satan will be loosed yet again, and he will fool many people into revolting against Christ (Revelation 20:7-9, NKJV). This is obviously a foolish idea, but the Bible tells us that it will happen; these people will attack Jesus and His saints, but will be destroyed by fire (Revelation 20:9-10, NKJV). The best way to avoid being a part of this group of people that are fooled by Satan is to be ready to meet Christ when He returns! If you are ready to meet Christ when He returns, you will be exempt from Satan's tricks and will be allied with Christ for eternity! God's Kingdom will be far superior in every way to any government that this world has ever experienced!

While many God ordained ministers will be preaching the gospel up until the very end of the Beast's reign, John tells of two specific men that will be mighty advocates for Jesus leading up to His return. John details their ministry will consist of a specific number of days in which they witness during the tribulation period: one thousand, two hundred, and sixty days (Revelation 11:3, NKJV). It is not by accident that this is approximately three and one-half years! Daniel, Paul, Mark, Matthew, and John are all talking about the same period of time! At the end of the second half of Daniel's week of years, Paul's forty-two months, and John's one thousand, two hundred, and sixty days, the seventh trumpet will sound! At this time, the Beast's reign will come to an abrupt end, Jesus Christ will reappear in the clouds, and all humans on earth, which have lived their lives for Christ, will lift off of this earth to meet Him in the air!

It is not coincidence that the Bible records a specific timeframe that will transpire just before Christ's return! God wants all of mankind to be ready to meet Him! He has provided a countdown for us in His Word, but it will only be visible to the children of light who remain awake and watchful! Since this book is intended to focus on Jesus, we have not discussed the first five trumpets; instead, we have primarily focused on the seventh trumpet, which announces the return of Christ! However, due to its significance, I feel compelled to briefly mention the sixth trumpet.

It is important to note that these trumpets sound in sequential order; therefore, the seventh trumpet will not sound before the sixth trumpet. As you have seen in previous paragraphs, the Bible gives specific timeframes for some prophecies, but does not clearly define the duration of time that will transpire between the sixth and seventh trumpets. However, the sixth trumpet will precede the seventh and will be glaringly obvious, which is why I feel a responsibility to mention it here. The sixth trumpet will be a global war, but not just any war. This war will be larger than any war that has ever been fought in the history of mankind. The Bible actually gives us the number of casualties that will be inflicted during this war; astonishingly, one-third of mankind will perish as a direct result of this war (Revelation 9:13-21, NKJV). John tells us that this war will begin in the vicinity of the Euphrates River (Revelation 9:14, NKJV). This river runs through Turkey, Syria, and Iraq, which have all been hot spots of conflict for many years. According to this prophecy, we see that at least one more conflict will arise from this area and it will be devastating. Due of the severe casualties that are inflicted during this war, it is evident that this war will include nuclear weapons.

The world population is currently just over seven and one-half billion people (United States Census Bureau, 2010). Even though this war begins in the vicinity of the Euphrates River, in order to accomplish such devastating casualties, many other nations must join this war, which includes nations that have nuclear capabilities. The highest number of casualties in any war came in World War II; this war claimed fifty-two million lives (Baxter, 2012). The largest war before that was World War I with just over eight million lives lost (Baxter, 2012). A war with two and one-half billion casualties is mind boggling; to imagine such a tragic loss of life is heart wrenching. The thought immediately comes to mind: What will be the eternal destination for all of those people? It breaks my heart for even one person to enter into eternity without salvation; this war will see one-third of all lives cut short. Undoubtedly many that lose their lives during this war will be ill-prepared to enter into eternity. The devastation of this war will be a catastrophe of epic proportions. The anticipation of this war should cause every person reading this book to take inventory of his or her life in order to ensure readiness to meet Christ. Due to the blatant nature of this trumpet, those that live through this war should be intimately aware that the only trumpet remaining is the one that announces Christ's return!

When God gave Daniel prophecies about the final seven years, Daniel prayed for God to reveal those prophecies to him; however, God told Daniel, "Go your way, Daniel, for the words are closed up and sealed till the time of the end" (Daniel 12:9, NKJV). God was telling Daniel that these prophecies will not be revealed until it is time for them to be revealed. God told Daniel that during the final seven years "none of the wicked shall understand, but the wise shall understand" (Daniel 12:10, NKJV). The wise will be able to recognize the global war that kills one-third of mankind, the seven year treaty involving Israel's ancestral homeland, the construction of the Third Jewish Temple, and the Abomination of Desolation, which will allow them to understand that God's countdown is nearing an end! As we discussed earlier, this was echoed when Paul talked about the sons of light versus those of darkness (1 Thessalonians 5:5, NKJV). God will not catch His people of light off guard because they will know Biblical prophecies and will watch as each unfolds.

Since prophecy is interpreted in accordance with God's timeclock, no matter how much time, energy, or prayer that is expended, God simply does not allow people to understand some prophecies until the designated time arrives. You may wonder: Why is this significant? It is significant because the designated time is here! God waited until the time just prior to His return before revealing some of His prophecies. God authored the Bible in such a way that only the people living during the final years of this age are able to understand some of His ancient prophecies! This knowledge was not intended for any other generation of people; God was specifically prophesying to us!

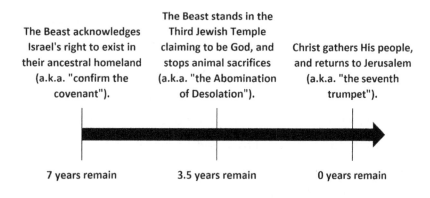

God's timeclock is winding down rapidly, and the generation that witnesses the Israeli and Palestinian peace agreement will also witness the return of Jesus Christ! Daniel prophesied that Christ will return seven years after the Beast openly displays his approval for God's covenant with Abraham concerning the land of Israel! During the vast majority of the final years, it will be difficult to ascertain an exact date of Christ's return because Daniel appears to only narrow it down to a forty-five day window (Daniel 12:11-12, KJV). However, the Bible gives us one final sign just before Christ returns that will be so clear that no one should miss it! God's two powerful witnesses will be preaching throughout the final years, but they will be murdered just three days prior to the return of Jesus Christ (Revelation 11:3-15, NKJV). It appears that news of their murder will be televised around the world. If you somehow miss every other sign in the Bible, do not miss this one! The bodies of these two men will lie in the streets of Jerusalem for three days, and then the seventh trumpet will sound, which will announce Christ's return!

> For the Lord Himself will descend from heaven with a shout, with the voice of an archangel, and with the trumpet of God. And the dead in Christ will rise first. (1 Thessalonians 4:16, NKJV)

> Now when He had spoken these things, while they watched, He was taken up, and a cloud received Him out of their sight. And while they looked steadfastly toward

heaven as He went up, behold, two men
stood by them in white apparel, who also
said, Men of Galilee, why do you stand
gazing up into heaven? This same Jesus,
who was taken up from you into heaven,
will so come in like manner as you saw Him
go into heaven. (Acts 1:9-11, NKJV)

At His second coming, Jesus will return to earth as the manifest presence of God in bodily form! As we discussed, this will occur at the seventh trumpet, which will be announced by Michael the archangel. Similarly to how Jesus Christ ascended into the heavens from Bethany, He will descend from the clouds on His way back to earth! There will be a mighty shout that will herald Christ's return, which will ring throughout the heavens! It will reverberate in our ears, and suddenly we will see the skies open up as a human Jesus moves steadily closer to earth. He will continue His descent until His feet touch down in Jerusalem, Israel. This return will mark the beginning of His rule as King of kings!

Behold, I tell you a mystery: We shall not
all sleep, but we shall all be changed—in a
moment, in the twinkling of an eye, at the
last trumpet. For the trumpet will sound,

and the dead will be raised incorruptible,
and we shall be changed. For this
corruptible must put on incorruption, and
this mortal must put on immortality. (1
Corinthians 15:51-53, NKJV)

At His second coming, Jesus will collect all of His people! The dead will come out of their graves, and both the living and dead will be changed from mortal to immortal in an instant! Paul tells us that our bodies will be transformed in a moment of time, which will be so rapid that it will be comparable to a "twinkling of an eye" (1 Corinthians 15:52, NKJV). One moment we will be mortal and a moment later we will be immortal! In this same verse, Paul goes on to tell us that this transformation will occur at the seventh trumpet (Endtime Blog, 2018).

Behold, the day of the Lord is coming, And
your spoil will be divided in your midst. For
I will gather all the nations to battle against
Jerusalem; The city shall be taken, The
houses rifled, And the women ravished.
Half of the city shall go into captivity, But
the remnant of the people shall not be cut
off from the city. Then the Lord will go
forth And fight against those nations, As He

fights in the day of battle. And in that day His feet will stand on the Mount of Olives, Which faces Jerusalem on the east. And the Mount of Olives shall be split in two, From east to west, Making a very large valley; Half of the mountain shall move toward the north And half of it toward the south. (Zechariah 14:1-4, NKJV)

So the angel thrust his sickle into the earth and gathered the vine of the earth, and threw it into the great winepress of the wrath of God. And the winepress was trampled outside the city, and blood came out of the winepress, up to the horses' bridles, for one thousand six hundred furlongs. (Revelation 14:19-20, NKJV)

Assemble and come, all you nations, And gather together all around. Cause Your mighty ones to go down there, O Lord. Let the nations be wakened, and come up to the Valley of Jehoshaphat; For there I will sit to judge all the surrounding nations. (Joel 3:11-12, NKJV)

Behold, I am coming as a thief. Blessed is
he who watches, and keeps his garments,
lest he walk naked and they see his shame.
And they gathered them together to the
place called in Hebrew, Armageddon.
(Revelation 16:15-16, NKJV)

At His second coming, Jesus will fight against the enemies of
Israel. The Beast and his unified world government army will
invade Israel from the north and march south towards
Jerusalem. One thousand and six hundred furlongs is about
one hundred and sixty miles (Endtime Magazine Articles,
2010). This is the approximate distance from Israel's northern
border in the Golan Heights, through Megiddo, and down to
Jerusalem. Israel will defend itself valiantly, but will be
outmatched by the Beast's global army. An intense and bloody
battle will be fought at Megiddo, which is where the armies
will assemble to fight the battle of Armageddon.

Israel will be steadily pushed southward and will ultimately
retreat as far south as Jerusalem. In Israel's most desperate
hour, just as defeat appears to be imminent, Jesus Christ will
descend from the clouds to fight on their behalf! Israel will be
on the brink of defeat, but Jesus will arrive on the scene to
vanquish wickedness from the earth! Jesus' feet will first touch

earth on the Mount of Olives, which is just outside of the old city of Jerusalem. Jesus Christ will join the war at the Kidron Valley, which is the valley that separates the Mount of Olives from the Temple Mount in Jerusalem. Joel lets us know that this battle will take place in the "Valley of Jehoshaphat" (Joel 3:12, NKJV). This valley is defined as: the Lord has judged (Easton, 1897). The Valley of Jehoshaphat and the Kidron Valley are synonymous terms for the same area on the eastern side of Jerusalem (Easton, 1897).

> And the armies in heaven, clothed in fine linen, white and clean, followed Him on white horses. (Revelation 19:14, NKJV)

> Blow the trumpet in Zion, And sound an alarm in My holy mountain! Let all the inhabitants of the land tremble; For the day of the Lord is coming, For it is at hand: A day of darkness and gloominess, A day of clouds and thick darkness, Like the morning clouds spread over the mountains. A people come, great and strong, The like of whom has never been; Nor will there ever be any such after them, Even for many successive generations. A

fire devours before them, And behind them a flame burns; The land is like the Garden of Eden before them, And behind them a desolate wilderness; Surely nothing shall escape them. Their appearance is like the appearance of horses; And like swift steeds, so they run. With a noise like chariots Over mountaintops they leap, Like the noise of a flaming fire that devours the stubble, Like a strong people set in battle array. Before them the people writhe in pain; All faces are drained of color. They run like mighty men, They climb the wall like men of war; Every one marches in formation, And they do not break ranks. They do not push one another; Every one marches in his own column. Though they lunge between the weapons, They are not cut down. They run to and fro in the city, They run on the wall; They climb into the houses, They enter at the windows like a thief. The earth quakes before them, The heavens tremble; The sun and moon grow dark, And the stars diminish their brightness. The Lord gives voice before His army, For His camp is very great; For strong

is the One who executes His word. For the
day of the Lord is great and very terrible;
Who can endure it? (Joel 2:1-11, NKJV)

The war we have been discussing is referred to in the Bible as the "great winepress of the wrath of God" (Revelation 14:19, NKJV). At first the casualties experienced by the world army will be inflicted by the Israeli military, but, once Christ enters the battle, the world army will be obliterated by God's army; His army will consist of His saints (Jude 1:14-15, KJV). John gives us a picture of so many soldiers dying during this war that the floor of the Kidron Valley will be covered in blood (Revelation 14:19-20, NKJV). John refers to the armies of heaven; this is the same group of human people that we spoke of earlier, which will be the people gathered by Christ from around the world (Revelation 19:14, NKJV). This gathering takes place just before they all descend upon the Mount of Olives to join in the battle. As we spoke earlier in this chapter, the saints of God will ascend into the clouds and meet Jesus as He is descending to earth. We also spoke earlier about people being transformed from mortal beings into immortal beings.

In the book of Joel, we get a glimpse of these new immortal bodies! Joel tells us, "For the day of the Lord is coming...A people come, great and strong...Their appearance is like the appearance of horses; And like swift steeds, so they run...Every one marches in his own column. Though they lunge between the weapons, They are not cut down...The Lord gives voice before His army, For His camp is very great...For the day of the Lord is great and very terrible; Who can endure it?" (Joel 2:1-11, NKJV) The people of God will be immortal and very mighty! The saints will execute war against the Beast and the world army without receiving any injuries! You might notice in Revelation that the saints are riding white horses, but in Joel they run as fast as horses. The references to horses are simply metaphors to explain the swift movement of God's army. The Beast and his army will be soundly defeated, and Jesus and His army will be unquestionably victorious! Jesus was a servant when He came to earth the first time, but will be the mighty victor at His second coming!

> Then I saw an angel coming down from
> heaven, having the key to the bottomless
> pit and a great chain in his hand. He laid
> hold of the dragon, that serpent of old,
> who is the Devil and Satan, and bound him
> for a thousand years; and he cast him into
> the bottomless pit, and shut him up, and
> set a seal on him, so that he should deceive
> the nations no more till the thousand years

were finished. But after these things he
must be released for a little while.
(Revelation 20:1-3, NKJV)

At His second coming, Jesus will bind Satan in chains for one thousand years! After the Beast and his army are defeated, Satan will be arrested and sentenced to one thousand years in a pit. The enemy of our souls will be powerless against us and life on earth will be perfect! John says that there will be no more deception while Satan is imprisoned; honesty and truth will prevail unchecked! In chapter four, we spoke about knowledge before and after Christ's return. We discussed how knowledge before Christ's return can be considered childish because it is so incomplete, but after Satan is imprisoned knowledge will no longer be diluted by Satan's lies. Knowledge will be solely based upon God's truth! Truth will be taught in schools, homes, and every social institution. Evolution, gender fluidity, murder of unborn children, and other lies will no longer be taught or accepted as truth! Knowledge will be solely based upon truth as authored by God. Good will finally triumph over evil and light over darkness! The King of Glory will become the eternal King over all!

Then I, John, saw the holy city, New Jerusalem, coming down out of heaven from God, prepared as a bride adorned for her husband. And I heard a loud voice from heaven saying, Behold, the tabernacle of God is with men, and He will dwell with them, and they shall be His people. God Himself will be with them and be their God. (Revelation 21:2-3, NKJV)

And I saw thrones, and they sat on them, and judgment was committed to them. Then I saw the souls of those who had been beheaded for their witness to Jesus and for the word of God, who had not worshiped the beast or his image, and had not received his mark on their foreheads or on their hands. And they lived and reigned with Christ for a thousand years. (Revelation 20:4, NKJV)

The wolf also shall dwell with the lamb, The leopard shall lie down with the young goat, The calf and the young lion and the fatling together; And a little child shall lead them. The cow and the bear shall graze;

Their young ones shall lie down together;
And the lion shall eat straw like the ox. The
nursing child shall play by the cobra's hole,
And the weaned child shall put his hand in
the viper's den. They shall not hurt nor
destroy in all My holy mountain, For the
earth shall be full of the knowledge of the
Lord As the waters cover the sea. (Isaiah
11:6-9, NKJV)

At His second coming, Jesus will establish an earthly Kingdom that will last for one thousand years! Mankind will be ruled by Jesus Christ Himself! The earth will finally experience a King whose kingdom covers the earth and causes complete peace and harmony. There will be no more violence or pain; even the animals will live in tranquility! Isaiah gives us a picture of perfect world peace. This world has always longed for peace, but will never truly experience it until Christ begins to reign in His Kingdom. Leopards, goats, cobras, cows, bears, lions, and oxen will all cohabitate in peace! Carnivores will become herbivores and fear will be a concept of the past!

The victory of Jesus is going to be one of the most celebrated and exciting moments in the history of earth! Satan will be defeated, and there will finally be peace on earth and goodwill towards all people! We will finally have a one world ruler that is not susceptible to greed, envy, perversion, selfishness, or malic! The heart of our King will be pure and undefiled! All creation will exist in perfect harmony! It is hard to fathom a world without suffering, death, pain, or sorrow! It seems too good to be true; a figment of our imagination! However, the prophecies of the Bible always come to pass. One day an imperfect world will be transformed into perfection!

How to Win

> I was watching; and the same horn was making war against the saints, and prevailing against them, until the Ancient of Days came, and a judgment was made in favor of the saints of the Most High, and the time came for the saints to possess the kingdom. (Daniel 7:21-22, NKJV)

> And I saw thrones, and they sat on them, and judgment was committed to them. Then I saw the souls of those who had been beheaded for their witness to Jesus and for the word of God, who had not worshiped the beast or his image, and had not received his mark on their foreheads or

on their hands. And they lived and reigned
with Christ for a thousand years.
(Revelation 20:4, NKJV)

Jesus has an offer we should not refuse! When He becomes
the supreme King, He will give leadership positions to a select
group of people. He is offering an opportunity to take part in
His victory! According to Daniel, only Jesus' saints are given
leadership of His Kingdom; therefore, in order to take part in
the millennial reign with Christ, we must live a life that is
consistent with the title of a saint (Daniel 7:22, NKJV). If we do
not achieve anything else in this life, we definitely want the
designation of saint! In order to become a saint of God, we
must complete two requirements: 1) have the Holy Spirit living
and residing inside of us; and, 2) allow the Holy Spirit to lead us
into all truth.

Before we discuss how to have the Holy Spirit reside within
us, we should look at why this is desirable. There are two major
reasons for having the Holy Spirit live within us: 1) to help us
live a life free from the bondage of sin; and, 2) to enable us to
take part in the physical resurrection! The physical resurrection
is the same event as our gathering together unto Jesus at His
return, which we discussed earlier in this chapter.

Do you not know that the unrighteous will not inherit the kingdom of God? Do not be deceived. Neither fornicators, nor idolaters, nor adulterers, nor homosexuals, nor sodomites, nor thieves, nor covetous, nor drunkards, nor revilers, nor extortioners will inherit the kingdom of God. And such were some of you. But you were washed, but you were sanctified, but you were justified in the name of the Lord Jesus and by the Spirit of our God. (1 Corinthians 6:9-11, NKJV)

Not by works of righteousness which we have done, but according to His mercy He saved us, through the washing of regeneration and renewing of the Holy Spirit. (Titus 3:5, NKJV)

Living a life free from sin is impossible without the Spirit of God. This is because our flesh loves to disobey God. Earlier in this book, we defined sin as humans using God's creation in a manner for which it was not designed. In chapter one, we defined righteousness as consistently doing that with is right in the eyes of God; we could also say that righteousness is using God's creation in a manner for which it was created! Since God is the Creator, He has the authority to instruct us in how to use His creation!

In the Bible, God's manual about His creation, God not only classifies actions that He deems to be right, but He also describes many actions that violate His plan. A righteous perspective is one that focuses on pleasing God, but sometimes we need a more blatant approach in order to learn how to avoid displeasing Him. Paul documented a few of these violations: fornication, idolatry, adultery, homosexuality, sodomy, thievery, covetousness, alcoholism, abuse, and extortion (1 Corinthians 6:9-10, NKJV). Homosexuality is a crass example of how humans attempt to misuse God's creation; adultery is another glaring example. God designed the human sexes to complement one another, and He designed marriage to consist of an unbreakable vow between one man and one woman. God not only created the people, places, and things of creation, but He intentionally designed all of them for a purpose! God intends for people, places, and things to be used in His own specific manner. The elementary nature of these concepts is obvious, but our enemy is attempting to redefine and repurpose even the simplest of God's designs.

Our flesh would love to embrace every opportunity to displease God because our flesh desires wickedness. It is our love of disobedience that causes us to derail and influences us to veer off of God's track. The desire we have to plot our own course or live by our own rules is known as our will. Jesus also had a rebellious human will; however, we must follow Jesus' example when He said, "Not my will, but Yours, be done" (Luke 22:42, NKJV). It is important that we verbalize this prayer as frequently as possible! If we were to analyze our life, can we honestly say that God's will is being accomplished through us? This prayer is a particularly difficult one to pray because it means we forgo our own will in lieu of His will. After all, what if His will includes something that we do not want to do? What if it includes going somewhere that we would rather not go?

I am certain that many parents have witnessed their child pretending to be a fireman, veterinarian, or doctor. This is because people begin anticipating their future from a very young age; anticipation gives way to expectation, which eventually turns into reality. Establishing dreams, planning the future, and executing those plans are perfectly normal activities. However, we must make sure that we arrive at His destination. We must examine the motivation that drives our goals. Realigning our goals with His is the best way to be certain that we are traveling in the correct direction!

Our goals are often generated in an attempt to establish a feeling of self-worth. We want to feel accomplishment, the satisfaction that accompanies success, the social status that results from recognized acumen, or the benefits of luxury. The root of our goals can be boiled down to worth; how much are we worth? This concept is important because if we derive our self-worth from our own accomplishments, we will become a slave to ourselves.

You will never be happy while trying to please yourself! You will be the most demanding task master that you have ever served. No boss will ever undervalue your accomplishments, demean your confidence, or treat you as poorly as you will treat yourself. You will work your whole life chasing your dreams, just to find out that your life is a nightmare of emptiness, guilt, and shame. This is why we must be cautious to set our goals based on how they align with the Kingdom of God! Praying God's will in our life and abandoning our own may be painful at first, but it is the only way to be chosen by God. God calls every person, but very few are chosen by Him (Matthew 22:14, KJV). This is because God leaves the answer up to us. We have the opportunity to opt in or out; we often exclude ourselves by our own response to Him. If we are not chosen by God, it is because our answer to His call is no. Living in God's will means our answer to God's call, in both the everyday and life altering decisions, is always yes!

Since we are born with our own innate human will, it is impossible for us to follow or even know the will of God unless we have help from God. Jesus called Him the "Helper", which is just another name for the Holy Spirit (John 14:16, NKJV). Having the Holy Spirit in our life helps us to know the will of God! To know the will of God, we must be full of the Spirit of God and pray for His guidance on a daily basis! As we learn the will of God and begin to apply it to our lives we start our transformation process! This resulting slow and steady transformation process is known as sanctification. Sanctification is a purification process that slowly removes disobedient actions and habits, and it replaces them with those that are positive and profitable. We are sanctified by the washing of regeneration and renewing of God's Spirit. A person that is filled with the Spirit of God can repent of his or her sins and incrementally seek to learn the ways of God each and every day. This is how we all are washed, regenerated, and renewed! Of ourselves, we are sinners, but through the Spirit of God living and working inside of us, we are made overcomers and victorious!

> But if the Spirit of Him who raised Jesus
> from the dead dwells in you, He who raised
> Christ from the dead will also give life to
> your mortal bodies through His Spirit who
> dwells in you. Therefore, brethren, we are

debtors—not to the flesh, to live according
to the flesh. For if you live according to the
flesh you will die; but if by the Spirit you
put to death the deeds of the body, you
will live. For as many as are led by the
Spirit of God, these are sons of God.
(Romans 8:11-14, NKJV)

Earlier we spoke about wanting the Spirit of God to reside inside of us in order to transform our mortal bodies. This simply means that we need the Holy Spirit living within us in order to change our bodies to an immortal state when Christ returns to collect His people. An immortal body is simply a body that cannot die. It was the Holy Spirit residing inside of Jesus Christ that caused Him to resurrect from the dead; we require that same Spirit to do that resurrection work within us when Christ returns. We spoke briefly about a title in the Bible called a saint. A saint is a person that is filled with the Spirit of God and living a life that is actively sanctified by His Spirit! Therefore, it could be said, the lifestyle of a saint is the defining characteristic that will cause someone to be a participant in the resurrection of Christ! Adversely, the absence of this lifestyle will preclude someone from participating in the resurrection of the saints. Without the Spirit of God living inside of us, we will be excluded from the resurrection of the saints, and we will be unknowledgeable with regard to living our lives in a manner that is pleasing to God. Having the Holy Spirit in our lives is absolutely critical to our eternity with Him!

There are four noteworthy benefits of making sure we meet the requirements to be classified as a saint when Christ returns: 1) saints will immediately go to be with Jesus when He returns, 2) saints will be soldiers in God's victorious army, 3) saints will be given a position in Jesus' earthly Kingdom, and 4) saints will be exempt from the final judgment.

> Then we who are alive and remain shall be caught up together with them in the clouds to meet the Lord in the air. And thus we shall always be with the Lord. (1 Thessalonians 4:17, NKJV)

Earlier we discussed that Jesus will "gather together His elect" when He returns to earth (Mark 13:27, NKJV). This is the same event we are discussing when we talk about saints immediately going to be with Jesus. Everything we do in life is preparing us for this moment. The moment Christ returns will be one of the happiest and most joyful moments in the lives of His saints, but, for those that are not ready to meet Christ, it

223

will be the saddest day to ever occur. The culmination of our lives will come down to one moment, and there will only be one question on the exam: Are we ready to meet Jesus? If our life qualifies us to be a saint then it was a success, but, if not, everything that was achieved will be worthless and without meaning. We do not want to miss out on this moment! This is one party to which we must ensure our invitation!

In order for our lives to have meaning, we must achieve goals that can be measured long after the human race has deceased. We must ensure that our legacy does not end at the point where eternity begins; a life is a precious resource that should not be squandered! Jesus spoke of this concept when He commanded us to store up treasures in heaven; He warned that hoarding earthly possessions during the course of life is a pointless endeavor (Matthew 6:19-22, KJV). What we accumulate on earth during life will have no significance to us after death. In terms of amassing treasure, gold and silver are typically good candidates, but Christ informs us that a treasure that can be stolen is worthless. The term *human capital* takes on a whole new meaning when we consider investing in Christ's Kingdom! The fruit of our labor will be sweet if we are able to enjoy it throughout eternity! What we accomplish in this life is only as valuable as its longevity; a durable treasure is one that expands Christ's Kingdom in both knowledge and number. We expand Christ's Kingdom in knowledge when we study, meditate upon, and communicate God's Word through voice and action; we expand Christ's Kingdom in number when people respond to God's Word in obedience. Saints of God are effective at amassing eternal treasure!

It is important to labor in God's Kingdom while the opportunity exists. Jesus warned that the window of opportunity will only remain open for a very short time; we are only able to work during our course of life (John 9:4, KJV). Our window is open while we have health in our body and breathe in our lungs! Unfortunately, people often become distracted and fail to establish good work habits in God's Kingdom. However, in order to have fruit, it is critical that we evaluate our habits, prune the unprofitable, and enhance that which has eternal value!

It is highly likely that you have become emotional at a sporting event, while watching a romantic movie, or during a heated argument; emotion is part of our human physiology. As a society, we classify certain emotional responses as acceptable while discouraging others. Starting as children, we learn to imitate acceptable patterns of behavior through observation and experience. There is significant societal pressure to utilize these acceptable patterns and suppress the unacceptable. For instance, we cheer following a touchdown, clap when a speaker finishes a speech, and raise our hand and voice to hail a taxi. However, we avoid raising our voice at a funeral, and we suppress urges to accost an annoying coworker. We are taught acceptable behavior from a very young age, which raises the question: Who is conditioning our behavior and should these boundaries ever be questioned? While many societal norms are appropriate, others can be detrimental!

Since we are evaluating behavior, it is important to understand what God likes and dislikes. Does God have an expected decorum? Does He frown upon exuberant behavior? These questions are answered in His Word. God does not value tradition, but He places a premium on sincerity and quality of relationship (Luke 10:27, KJV). Notice in this verse how Jesus says we are to love Him: "love the Lord thy God with all thy heart, and with all thy soul, and with all thy strength, and with all thy mind." If we love Him with our actions, but without heart then it is not love. If we love Him with our heart, but fail to follow through with action then it is not love. Loving God is all or nothing! We often allow tradition to dictate how we act towards God, but tradition does not impress Him. Our kneeling, standing, or moving around does nothing to enhance our relationship with God unless those movements are accompanied by emotion for Him! Nothing can separate us from God's love; He will always love us! When we love God through obedience, we ensure that God is not separated from our love (John 14:21, NKJV). When we forgo tradition and opt for obedience, we get the attention of God! Outward expression is love by strength, emotion is love by heart, continuing daily is love by life, and prayer, study of God's Word, and meditation is love by mind. We are commanded to love through obedience!

Can you imagine a mother or father that refuse to show affection to their child? What if a husband or wife withheld emotion from one another? In this instance, the result would likely be a failed marriage. Do you think treating God the same way would have a different outcome? We may not call it a divorce, but separating and isolating God by refusing to show affection is just as real! We divorce God by failing to love Him!

Outward expression is an expected response when it comes to our relationship with God! Emotion should be a natural part of our conversation with God! It was David that danced before the Lord when he returned with the Ark of the Covenant (2 Samuel 6:14-15, NKJV). Hannah wept before God when she prayed for a son (1 Samuel 1:10, KJV). The Israelites sacrificed in their new Temple with joy after returning to Jerusalem from captivity (Ezra 6:15-17, KJV). We are expected to praise God with sound, effort, and emotion (Psalm 150:1-6, KJV). God loves us and He loves our emotion! Building a relationship with God is investing eternal treasure! Saints praise and worship their God out of love and admiration for Him! Praise is a requirement now because it will be a privilege throughout eternity! This is why we love Him with heart, strength, life, and mind!

I do not wish to contradict a concept we discussed in chapter three of this book, but I feel compelled to point out one exception. It is true that mortal humans will exist in eternity as immortal humans, which is how Jesus exists at this very moment! However, there is an exception to this rule for people who die before the return of Christ. When Christ returns, His saints that predeceased His return will be the first to resurrect from their graves, which means their spirit will be reunited with an immortal version of their bodies (1 Thessalonians 4:16-17, NKJV). The gap of time between death and resurrection is where we encounter the exception.

When saints die they go into a resting state until the resurrection; they exist in a pseudo-physical state until they are given an immortal body, which John described as "white robes" (Revelation 6:9-11, KJV). At death, physical bodies cease to house the spirit and the lifeless flesh returns to dust (Genesis 3:19, KJV). However, the spirit and soul of dead saints are not given a fully immortal body until Christ returns to earth; Paul describes this event when he says, "the Lord Himself will descend from heaven with a shout, with the voice of an archangel, and with the trumpet of God. And the dead in Christ will rise first. Then we who are alive and remain shall be caught up together with them in the clouds to meet the Lord in the air." (1 Thessalonians 4:16-17, NKJV).

If God's saints receive an immortal body, what about people who are not saints? Do unsaved people live throughout eternity with an immortal body? Jesus answered this question with a story of a rich man that died and found himself separated from God; while in this eternal state, he asked for a drop of water to cool his tongue (Luke 16:24, KJV). If non-saints have tongues in eternity, we can infer that the rest of the body will also exist. We must also flesh out what it means to have an eternal existence away from Christ.

Since the first benefit of being a saint involves living with God for eternity, this insinuates there must be an alternate eternal existence away from God. This existence away from God is explained by John as eternal torment, which is reserved for people that pledge allegiance to the Beast by taking the mark of the Beast (Revelation 14:10-11, KJV). John also describes this state as a "second death" that consists of burning in molten lava (Revelation 21:8, NKJV). In this verse, the list of inhabitants is extended to include people that have not repented from sinful acts such as lying, fornication, murder, idolatry, and witchcraft; however, it is not isolated to these sins because it also identifies people that do not believe in Christ. The concept outlined above is consistent with the story Jesus told about the rich man desiring water to cool his tongue, and it aligns with other instances where fire is referenced (James 3:6; Mark 9:47-48, KJV). Jesus refers to this location designed for eternal torment as "hell"; He tells us to reverence the One that has the power to not only cause death, but also has the authority to sentence to hell (Luke 12:4-5, KJV). Anyone that does not qualify as a saint of God will reap the ghastly fate that accompanies an eternal existence separated from God.

This is not a topic to ignore or minimize; eternity is a reality, and God only affords us two options. Each destination is optional, predicated upon our life choices. We have the option of loving and serving God or hating and opposing God. There is no middle ground, no in-between, and no gray area. The destination rests soundly in our control; we have the freedom to willingly choose the path we take. Each day we step out of bed, we have to address this eternal question. Every day we answer God with either a yes or no, but these opportunities only remain as long as we continue stepping out of bed each morning. In our future, a day will come when the question will no longer be raised; the option will no longer be posed. On this day, we will lock in our decision one final time.

> And have made us kings and priests to our
> God; And we shall reign on the earth.
> (Revelation 5:10, NKJV)

We have already discussed the role that the saints will play during the final battle on earth. The saints will be God's heavenly army that defeats the Beast and his global army. We definitely want to be on the winning side of this war! Since we have already discussed this benefit, we will move on to the third benefit of being a saint. Christ will establish a Kingdom here on earth, which will last for one thousand years. Being a saint of God will qualify us for a position in His Kingdom! We will be able to occupy roles of authority in God's government, and we will rule over the mortal people that remain on the earth for the duration of Christ's Kingdom. The saints will be immortal, which means they will never experience death; only perpetual life in God's Kingdom of joy and peace!

> But the rest of the dead did not live again
> until the thousand years were finished.
> This is the first resurrection. Blessed and
> holy is he who has part in the first

resurrection. Over such the second death has no power, but they shall be priests of God and of Christ, and shall reign with Him a thousand years. (Revelation 20:5-6, NKJV)

Then I saw a great white throne and Him who sat on it, from whose face the earth and the heaven fled away. And there was found no place for them. And I saw the dead, small and great, standing before God, and books were opened. And another book was opened, which is the Book of Life. And the dead were judged according to their works, by the things which were written in the books. The sea gave up the dead who were in it, and Death and Hades delivered up the dead who were in them. And they were judged, each one according to his works. Then Death and Hades were cast into the lake of fire. This is the second death. And anyone not found written in the Book of Life was cast into the lake of fire. (Revelation 20:11-15, NKJV)

When the Son of Man comes in His glory,
and all the holy angels with Him, then He
will sit on the throne of His glory. All the
nations will be gathered before Him, and
He will separate them one from another,
as a shepherd divides his sheep from the
goats. And He will set the sheep on His
right hand, but the goats on the left. Then
the King will say to those on His right hand,
Come, you blessed of My Father, inherit
the kingdom prepared for you from the
foundation of the world. (Matthew 25:31-
34, NKJV)

The mortal people that are not gathered at the resurrection of the saints and remain alive on earth after the final war, will continue to live in Christ's earthly Kingdom. The people that are dead when Christ returns will remain in their graves until the end of Christ's millennial Kingdom. After the thousand year reign of Christ draws to a close, all humanity will stand before Christ to answer for the words and actions that accumulated during their lives. Standing before Christ at the end of time is the final judgment, which is also called the second death. This leads us to our final benefit of being a saint, which is exemption from the final judgment. John said, "Blessed and holy is he who has part in the first resurrection. Over such the second death has no power" (Revelation 20:6, NKJV). It is possible that saints will be in attendance when all humanity is judged by Christ; however, judgment will not be rendered against the saints because they will have already passed their first exam! At this point, their names will have already been recorded in the book of life and their sins forever washed away. They will have been filled with the Spirit of God and washed, regenerated, and renewed! They will be found faithful to Christ; therefore, the final judgment will only be a formality. It may be similar to a pinning ceremony, but none of the saints will be excluded from eternal life with God. These people will only hear, "Come, you blessed of My Father, inherit the kingdom prepared for you from the foundation of the world" (Matthew 25:34, NKJV). You see this is why every human was created! We were all meant to be in a relationship with God! Every human is intended to enter into everlasting life with God, but wickedness separates us from Him. He beckons us to come back to Him and allow Him to cover our sins with His blood. He longs for us to make our hearts right and remediate the debt we accrue through sin. He is waiting for us to accept His offer, and He is ready to pay our debt, if only we will ask Him!

In this chapter, we discussed Jesus as the head of God, and how He has all power and dominion over heaven and earth.

We also discussed the significance of the manifestation of the human Jesus and why God chose to utilize this manifestation. Finally, we discussed the importance of following the perfect example that Jesus gave us and the significance of being classified as a saint. Due to the vital and eternal importance, we will summarize this last point one more time. Without the Holy Spirit dwelling in and directing our lives, Jesus will not recognize us as His saints, and our names will not be written in His book of life! There is no immediate, carnal gratification that is valuable enough to forego the eternal benefits of being a saint of the most High! You and I want to ensure that we are part of His Kingdom every step of the way because victory belongs to Jesus! Jesus defeated sin, and He will fulfill His purpose at the final judgment as He casts Satan into the lake of fire. It is paramount that we avoid this terrible destination; instead, we must make it our life goal to spend all eternity with Jesus!

> And He Himself gave some to be apostles,
> some prophets, some evangelists, and
> some pastors and teachers, for the
> equipping of the saints for the work of
> ministry, for the edifying of the body of
> Christ. (Ephesians 4:11-12, NKJV)

God gifts people with various talents; Paul informs us that some people have a gift of prophecy, which is endowed by God (Ephesians 4:11-12, NKJV). It is important to follow the correct voice when seeking to understand the prophecies of the Bible, and there are many false voices vying for our attention! Some will intentionally mislead, others will unwittingly portray a false narrative, but a select few will properly interpret the prophecies found in God's Word! God is the only one that can both seal and reveal His prophecy; and His method is often to reveal it in His own time through His prophets. Be certain that the voice to which you listen is the voice of truth! Some seek to understand Biblical prophecy through intellect and deduction alone, but a prophet will rely on revelation from Almighty God. Be prayerful and selective when believing someone's interpretation of Biblical prophecy!

As I draw this chapter to a close, I would like to offer words of appreciation as a memorial to a phenomenal prophet in my life. The Bible tells us that God ordains teachers, evangelists, apostles, pastors, and prophets. I have been blessed to learn from a prophet ordained of God. I was first introduced to Prophet Irvin Baxter's teachings in 2014 by my friend Reverend Terry Freeman. I never had the privilege of meeting Prophet Baxter in person; nevertheless, he was an integral contributor to my life, a meaningful influencer in my ministry, and a wonderful source of knowledge through the years. I deeply appreciate and value his contributions to the Kingdom of God while he was alive. Prophet Irvin Baxter passed from this life due to complications related to the Novel Coronavirus on November 3, 2020; he is greatly missed and will be fondly remembered!

SIX

The Temple of God

The Torn Veil

In chapter five, we discussed why we want the Holy Spirit in our lives. In this chapter, we will take a more in-depth look at the temple of God and the method by which we invite His Spirit to live within us!

> That the king said unto Nathan the prophet, See now, I dwell in an house of cedar, but the ark of God dwelleth within curtains. And Nathan said to the king, Go, do all that is in thine heart; for the Lord is with thee. And it came to pass that night, that the word of the Lord came unto Nathan, saying, Go and tell my servant David, Thus saith the Lord, Shalt thou build

me an house for me to dwell in? Whereas I
have not dwelt in any house since the time
that I brought up the children of Israel out
of Egypt, even to this day, but have walked
in a tent and in a tabernacle. (2 Samuel
7:2-6, KJV)

Now on the day that the tabernacle was
raised up, the cloud covered the
tabernacle, the tent of the Testimony;
from evening until morning it was above
the tabernacle like the appearance of fire.
(Numbers 9:15, NKJV)

And Moses took the tabernacle, and
pitched it without the camp, afar off from
the camp, and called it the Tabernacle of
the congregation. And it came to pass, that
every one which sought the Lord went out
unto the tabernacle of the congregation,
which was without the camp. (Exodus 33:7,
KJV)

In chapter one, we discussed many attributes of God, two of
which were His invisibility and omnipresence. Since God exists
everywhere as an invisible Spirit, He cannot be confined into a

physical temple or location. As we previously discussed, this is because God is larger than His creation. Even though God will not fit in any edifice, it has not stopped people from trying to build structures to house God. David desired to build a house for God; God's response was enlightening! God told David that He has never lived in a house, but has only "walked in a tent and in a tabernacle" (2 Samuel 7:6, KJV). This is the Old Testament way of saying God manifested His invisible, omnipresent Spirit in and around the Jewish tabernacle. The priests interacted with God in the tabernacle; God also manifested Himself as a cloud that would cover the tabernacle in the day and as a fire that would be upon the tabernacle at night. To see God display Himself by perpetual fire must have been an amazing sight!

I have always been fascinated by fire. As a child, I could be found around any campfire watching and fueling the flames; adding small sticks and grass just to observe them burn. I can only imagine how the Israelites would gaze upon His wonder in amazement! The flames of God engulfing a tabernacle made of combustible materials; yet none of it was singed or scorched! God's presence would fill a manmade structure just for the benefit of mankind. He did not enter into the building for shelter or lodging! God wants so badly to have a relationship with His creation that He goes to extraordinary lengths in order to get our attention! However, a cloud in the day and a fire in the night were not the complete fullness of God; these were only visible manifestations that He utilized. God uses manifestations in order to let mankind know that He exists and desires companionship. The tabernacle did not keep rain or wind off of God; it was simply a location Jews could assemble in order to meet with God! Moses recorded that "every one which sought the Lord went out unto the tabernacle of the congregation, which was without the camp" (Exodus 33:7, KJV). People need a way to communicate with God; we need something to hear, see, or feel. This is why God would manifest Himself in manmade structures, so humans would know how to reach Him!

> And Jesus cried out again with a loud voice, and yielded up His spirit. Then, behold, the veil of the temple was torn in two from top to bottom; and the earth quaked, and the rocks were split. (Matthew 27:50-51, NKJV)

> Do you not know that you are the temple of God and that the Spirit of God dwells in you? (1 Corinthians 3:16, NKJV)

And I will pray the Father, and He will give
you another Helper, that He may abide
with you forever— the Spirit of truth,
whom the world cannot receive, because it
neither sees Him nor knows Him; but you
know Him, for He dwells with you and will
be in you. I will not leave you orphans; I
will come to you. (John 14:16-18, NKJV)

After Jesus died on the cross, the veil in the temple was
supernaturally ripped from top to bottom. The veil in the
temple signified a separation between human carnality and
God's holiness. Before going behind the veil to enter into the
presence of God, priests would go through a ritualistic
cleansing process. This procedure was required because God is
holy and every human has sinned against God. By tearing the
temple veil, God signified that He would no longer manifest
Himself in buildings or structures! Instead, He had something
much different in mind! Christ said, while talking to His
disciples, I dwell with you and I shall dwell in you (John 14:18,
NKJV). Paul tells us that our bodies are the temple of God (1
Corinthians 3:16, NKJV). God created an internal manifestation
in order to participate in our lives; He wants a personal,
intimate relationship with each and every one of us! Our
bodies have become the temple of our Lord!

The Invitation

> Behold, I stand at the door and knock. If
> anyone hears My voice and opens the
> door, I will come in to him and dine with
> him, and he with Me. (Revelation 3:20,
> NKJV)

> I will give you a new heart and put a new
> spirit within you; I will take the heart of
> stone out of your flesh and give you a
> heart of flesh. (Ezekiel 36:26, NKJV)

It is important to know that God is a perfect gentleman; He requires an invitation before He will take up residence in our temple. John shows us that God will not enter a door that is shut; we must invite the Holy Spirit to live in our earthly bodies (Revelation 3:20, NKJV). He will not intrude upon us until it is time for His second coming to earth! He will only knock on our heart's door hoping that we will allow Him to enter! Ezekiel recorded that, when the door is opened to God's Spirit, He will take our stony heart and replace it with a soft heart (Ezekiel 36:26, NKJV). Our thoughts, ambitions, hesitancies, biases, prejudices, selfishness, and hatred will be extracted and replaced with love! When our bodies become the temple of

God, we begin to resemble Him. Our thoughts, words, and actions begin to transform into His thoughts, words, and actions. It is not by our power, but by His power that our temples become clean!

Knowing how the Bible is laid out helps us understand where to look for instruction on how to invite the Holy Spirit to reside within us. The first four books of the New Testament are: Matthew, Mark, Luke, and John. These four books are known as the gospels; they chronicle the life of Jesus and document instruction He provided to His disciples. The instruction Jesus gave His disciples was intended to help them after He was gone. He taught them how they should live and what they should do after His death. The book of Acts, which is the fifth book of the New Testament, is where the disciples obeyed Christ's teachings and followed through with His instructions. The remainder of the New Testament is primarily directed towards instructing the saints on how to continue living a Godly life after the Holy Spirit takes up residence. This is also where we find explanation to explain why this type of life is so desirable. Obviously there are some overlapping themes, but this is a high level grouping of the New Testament. One consistent theme that can be found throughout the Bible is prophecy. Much of the Bible includes prophecy, but this category can be classified along with the *how* and *why* of living a life for Christ. It is important to get a full picture of what we must do to invite God to live within us. We must begin in the gospels in order to establish a baseline of Jesus' commandments; after we see what Jesus commanded, we should look at how His commandments were followed in the Acts of the Apostles.

> Jesus answered, Most assuredly, I say to
> you, unless one is born of water and the
> Spirit, he cannot enter the kingdom of God.
> (John 3:5, NKJV)

Jesus gave Nicodemus a high level overview of how to enter God's Kingdom by saying there is a physical baptism and a spiritual baptism required for salvation. It is impossible to enter into the Kingdom of God unless we are submerged in water in a physical rebirth and filled with His Spirit in a spiritual rebirth. Jesus used a metaphor that is familiar to all mankind, which is the birthing process. It is through birth that a new human will enter into the world. This young baby is a fledgling and incapable of life without a regular, steady diet of food. The food a baby eats is much different than that of an adult, and the baby is dependent upon others to sustain his or her life. Jesus tells us that if we want to enter into the Kingdom of God, we must be born into it. Every newborn Christian will go through a growing and maturing process. After a spiritual birth, the newborn Christian will struggle, fall down, learn to walk, grow, and learn. The growing and learning process is facilitated by the Spirit that took up residence in the newborn Christian after Spirit baptism. However, before someone can run he or she must crawl and before crawling he or she must first be born.

In the last paragraph, we spoke about not being able to enter into the Kingdom of God without undergoing a new birth process, but people may wonder: What is the Kingdom of God and why do I want to be a part of it? It is true that Christ will establish a physical Kingdom here on earth after His return; however, the Kingdom of God is more than an earthly government! The Kingdom of God is a way of life that consists of righteousness, peace, and joy (Romans 14:17, KJV). This way of life is consistent with how Jesus Christ lives His life, and it is a requirement if we want to be like Christ. The new birth process is an initial step into this Kingdom of God lifestyle, which teaches us how to live a life of righteousness, peace, and joy. It is this lifestyle that solidifies our residence in Christ's earthly Kingdom.

> And that repentance and remission of sins
> should be preached in His name to all
> nations, beginning at Jerusalem. (Luke
> 24:47, NKJV)

Just after His resurrection, Jesus told His disciples to preach repentance. Repentance is the first step in the new birth. This is because in order to be born spiritually, we have to hand over control of our lives to God. Everyone that has controlled their own destiny has made a mess of their lives. We steer ourselves into perilous waters instead of seeking the safety of a harbor. As captains of our lives, we are inept. Turning over control of our lives means that we admit our inabilities and confess our mistakes. If we confess our sins and turn control over to Him, God will forgive our trespasses. Repentance is a dying of the old captain and a releasing of the helm in order to relinquish control. The old captain may try to reinstate his authority, but a dead man tells no tales; make sure the old man is dead! Your will and God's will are adverse to one another; therefore, we are unable to lead ourselves into God's harbor!

> And He said to them, Go into all the world
> and preach the gospel to every creature.
> He who believes and is baptized will be
> saved; but he who does not believe will be

248

condemned. And these signs will follow
those who believe: In My name they will
cast out demons; they will speak with new
tongues. (Mark 16:15-17, NKJV)

Just after His resurrection, Jesus told His disciples to preach
baptism. It is the preaching of the gospel that leads to belief
and baptism. Jesus said if people believe the message of the
gospel then they will be baptized, but if they do not believe
then there will be a very undesirable result. Jesus told
Nicodemus that he could not enter into the Kingdom of God
unless he is first baptized; Jesus builds on that statement by
saying, "He who believes and is baptized will be saved; but he
who does not believe will be condemned" (Mark 16:16, NKJV).
Belief in Jesus and baptism in the name of Jesus is so critical
that failing to so will preclude us from an eternity with Christ!

He who believes in Me, as the Scripture
has said, out of his heart will flow rivers of
living water. But this He spoke concerning
the Spirit, whom those believing in Him
would receive; for the Holy Spirit was not
yet given, because Jesus was not yet
glorified. (John 7:38-39, NKJV)

I will not leave you orphans; I will come to you. A little while longer and the world will see Me no more, but you will see Me. Because I live, you will live also. At that day you will know that I am in My Father, and you in Me, and I in you. (John 14:18-20, NKJV)

Behold, I send the Promise of My Father upon you; but tarry in the city of Jerusalem until you are endued with power from on high. (Luke 24:49, NKJV)

And being assembled together with them, He commanded them not to depart from Jerusalem, but to wait for the Promise of the Father, which, He said, you have heard from Me; for John truly baptized with water, but you shall be baptized with the Holy Spirit not many days from now. (Acts 1:4-5, NKJV)

Just before His ascension into heaven, Christ told His disciples to go to Jerusalem and wait for the infilling of the Holy Spirit; He called it the "Promise of My Father" (Luke 24:49, NKJV). In order to complete the new birth, we must follow through with both a baptism of water and a baptism of God's Spirit. Jesus said, "Because I live, you will live also" (John 14:19, NKJV). When Jesus died He made a way of escape for us. We were talking about the ship captain earlier, abdicating the controls will only leave a ship without a captain; however, inviting a new captain to control the helm will ensure our destination! In the previous paragraph, we spoke about water baptism; now we are talking about the final birth. This is the moment a spiritual new man or woman emerges from birth. This happens at the baptism of the Holy Spirit. It is not just a spiritual baptism; it is a baptism of the Spirit of God. Get a mental image of someone being completely submerged and inundated in the Spirit of Almighty God! In order to complete the birthing process, we must have His Spirit!

Invitation Accepted

> Then they returned to Jerusalem from the mount called Olivet, which is near Jerusalem, a Sabbath day's journey. And when they had entered, they went up into the upper room where they were staying: Peter, James, John, and Andrew; Philip and Thomas; Bartholomew and Matthew; James the son of Alphaeus and Simon the

Zealot; and Judas the son of James. These
all continued with one accord in prayer and
supplication, with the women and Mary
the mother of Jesus, and with His brothers.
(Acts 1:12-14, NKJV)

And they were all filled with the Holy Spirit
and began to speak with other tongues, as
the Spirit gave them utterance. (Acts 2:4,
NKJV)

The disciples received the Holy Spirit while waiting in
Jerusalem. Jesus told His disciples, "Tarry in the city of
Jerusalem until you are endued with power from on high"
(Luke 24:49, NKJV). Luke also recorded, "Then they returned to
Jerusalem... These all continued with one accord in prayer and
supplication... And they were all filled with the Holy Spirit and
began to speak with other tongues, as the Spirit gave them
utterance" (Acts 1:12-14; 2:4, NKJV). This is the Spirit baptism!
The disciples obeyed the commandment of Jesus, prepared
themselves, and were baptized by the Spirit of God! The words
to Nicodemus were fulfilled, which is how the Holy Spirit of
God began to reside in the temple made by the hands of God.
Mankind was redeemed back to God, and we are no longer
separated from Him by a temple veil! We no longer have to

walk outside of the city seeking relationship with God through a tabernacle! We no longer have to send a priest into the Temple on our behalf! The fire that saturated the tabernacle came to dwell inside of mankind! Now we all can be saturated by and filled with the fire of God!

> Then Peter said to them, Repent, and let
> every one of you be baptized in the name
> of Jesus Christ for the remission of sins;
> and you shall receive the gift of the Holy
> Spirit. For the promise is to you and to your
> children, and to all who are afar off, as
> many as the Lord our God will call. (Acts
> 2:38-39, NKJV)

Peter summarizes how we are to invite the Holy Spirit to dwell within our temple. The new birthing process was finally summarized into a single coherent command. We do not have to decipher the new birth from multiple reference points in the Bible. Peter informs all people to, "Repent, and let every one of you be baptized in the name of Jesus Christ for the remission of sins; and you shall receive the gift of the Holy Spirit" (Acts 2:38, NKJV). In other words, we should give control over to the One that knows the journey of salvation and be reborn as a baby in Christ! This is how everyone should submit their invitation to the Holy Spirit; if we properly invite Him, we have a promise from God that we will be filled! Peter said, "For the promise is to you and to your children, and to all who are afar off" (Acts 2:39, NKJV). In other words, Peter is saying this promise that Jesus told me about is also promised to everyone else! There is no regard to age, gender, nationality, or social status! You just have to want it, do what the disciples did, and it will be yours! Jesus gave us a promise, "He who believes in Me, as the Scripture has said, out of his heart will flow rivers of living water" (John 7:38, NKJV). Both Peter and Jesus referenced the same promise, which is still available to us today!

> While Peter was still speaking these words, the Holy Spirit fell upon all those who heard the word. And those of the circumcision who believed were astonished, as many as came with Peter, because the gift of the Holy Spirit had been poured out on the Gentiles also. For they heard them speak with tongues and magnify God. Then Peter answered, Can anyone forbid water, that these should not be baptized who have received the Holy Spirit just as we have? And he commanded them to be baptized in the name of the

Lord. Then they asked him to stay a few
days. (Acts 10:44-48, NKJV)

The gentiles, or non-Jews, received the Holy Spirit in the
same manner as the disciples! Peter proclaimed that Jesus'
promise was for everyone, and, unsurprisingly, others were
also baptized in the Spirit of God! Luke recorded, "The gift of
the Holy Spirit had been poured out on the Gentiles also. For
they heard them speak with tongues and magnify God...who
have received the Holy Spirit just as we have" (Acts 10:45-47,
NKJV). The disciples recognized that the gentiles had been
baptized with the Spirit of God because they heard it! The
Spirit baptism is always accompanied by proof. No one has to
wonder if they have experienced Spirit baptism because it will
be accompanied by an unfamiliar language spoken by the
recipient. Paul calls this proof a sign that helps bring faith to
the unbeliever (1 Corinthians 14:22, NKJV). Absent proof,
people are unable to definitively know whether or not the Holy
Spirit has filled them. This is why God chose to provide a sign!

> He said to them, Did you receive the Holy
> Spirit when you believed? So they said to
> him, We have not so much as heard
> whether there is a Holy Spirit. And he said
> to them, Into what then were you

baptized? So they said, Into John's
baptism. Then Paul said, John indeed
baptized with a baptism of repentance,
saying to the people that they should
believe on Him who would come after him,
that is, on Christ Jesus. When they heard
this, they were baptized in the name of the
Lord Jesus. And when Paul had laid hands
on them, the Holy Spirit came upon them,
and they spoke with tongues and
prophesied. (Acts 19:2-6, NKJV)

The book of Acts includes stories that occurred over a
period of time that spans for many years; it covers
approximately thirty to forty years (Zondervan Academic Blog,
2018). In the book of Acts, Luke conveys stories that occurred
during the early years of the church. As you can see from our
discussions, some of these stories include events where people
were filled with the Holy Spirit. It is important to understand
that these Spirit baptisms occurred over several decades of
time; they did not all occur at one point in time. Another one
of these stories is where Paul encounters twelve men that
previously were disciples of John the Baptist. Paul asked, "Did
you receive the Holy Spirit when you believed?" (Acts 19:2,
NKJV) These men were unaware of the Holy Spirit, but gladly

followed the instruction of Paul. Paul instructed these followers of John the Baptist to be re-baptized in the name of Jesus; Luke records that they were also filled with the Holy Spirit. He stated, "They were baptized in the name of the Lord Jesus. And when Paul had laid hands on them, the Holy Spirit came upon them, and they spoke with tongues" (Acts 19:5-6, NKJV). The baptism of the Spirit of God is still available to every person that desires to have it! After Christ's resurrection, it was available for decades while the Bible was still being written, and it is still available to this very day!

In the Gospels, Jesus told His disciples what to do in order to invite the Holy Spirit to dwell within them. We see in the book of Acts that the disciples followed through with these commandments, and they passed these words on to many people with which they came in contact. Peter consolidated all elements, or steps, to the plan of salvation required to invite the Holy Spirit into our lives (Acts 2:38, NKJV). He went on to witness many people follow through with this plan of salvation! When we invite God to dwell within us, how do we know whether or not He accepted our invitation? The Bible tells us we will know by the evidence of vocal speech in an unfamiliar language. A language that is not our native tongue will begin to flow from our lips! It is definitive proof of baptism in the Spirit of God! This is the sign God chose as proof of God's acceptance to our invitation!

> Indeed it came to pass, when the trumpeters and singers were as one, to make one sound to be heard in praising and thanking the Lord, and when they lifted up their voice with the trumpets and cymbals and instruments of music, and praised the Lord, saying: For He is good, For His mercy endures forever, that the house, the house of the Lord, was filled with a cloud, so that the priests could not continue ministering because of the cloud; for the glory of the Lord filled the house of God. (2 Chronicles 5:13-14, NKJV)

> Then Solomon spoke: The Lord said He would dwell in the dark cloud. I have surely built You an exalted house, And a place for You to dwell in forever. Then the king turned around and blessed the whole assembly of Israel, while all the assembly of Israel was standing. And he said: Blessed be the Lord God of Israel, who has fulfilled with His hands what He spoke with His

mouth to my father David, saying, Since
the day that I brought My people out of
the land of Egypt, I have chosen no city
from any tribe of Israel in which to build a
house, that My name might be there, nor
did I choose any man to be a ruler over My
people Israel. Yet I have chosen Jerusalem,
that My name may be there, and I have
chosen David to be over My people Israel.
(2 Chronicles 6:1-6, NKJV)

Others mocking said, They are full of new
wine. But Peter, standing up with the
eleven, raised his voice and said to them,
Men of Judea and all who dwell in
Jerusalem, let this be known to you, and
heed my words. For these are not drunk, as
you suppose, since it is only the third hour
of the day. But this is what was spoken by
the prophet Joel: And it shall come to pass
in the last days, says God, That I will pour
out of My Spirit on all flesh; Your sons and
your daughters shall prophesy, Your young
men shall see visions, Your old men shall
dream dreams. And on My menservants
and on My maidservants I will pour out My

Spirit in those days; And they shall
prophesy. (Acts 2:13-18, NKJV)

In chapter three, we spoke about inheriting the name of
God. If you remember, we discussed how Christ inherited the
name of God when the Spirit of God took up residence in His
body; this took place when He was formed in Mary's womb.
We also discussed how each and every human has the
opportunity to be adopted into the family of God, and we do
this by being filled with the Spirit of God! Just like Jesus Christ,
we have an opportunity to take on His name and become a
joint-heir with Him! If you remember, joint-heir means we
inherit what Christ inherits. When King Solomon built the first
temple to God in Jerusalem, we see that God chose to place
His name on that temple. He did this after He began to dwell in
the temple!

The story of how the temple was dedicated after its
completion is quite fascinating! The Israelites were praising
God, singing, and playing music; at this moment, God's
presence filled the Temple in such a way that people were not
even able to stand up! This event is recorded as, "The
house...was filled with a cloud, so that the priests could not
continue ministering...for the glory of the Lord filled the house
of God" (2 Chronicles 5:13-14, NKJV). The writer goes on to say,

"I have chosen Jerusalem, that My name may be there" (2 Chronicles 6:6, NKJV). God only chose to place His name on the temple in Jerusalem after His Spirit filled that temple! You might wonder: Why is this significant to us today? This foreshadowing exemplifies the point at which humans, the new temple of God, receive the name of God!

If you compare the outpouring of God's spirit in Solomon's Temple to the outpouring of God's Spirit on the day of Pentecost, they are strikingly similar (2 Chronicles 6:6; Acts 2:1-13, NKJV). God is moved by the emotion and attention of mankind. At the first temple dedication, we see people praising and worshiping God as His Spirit began to move over them; similarly, at the feast of Pentecost, the disciples were gathered in prayer when God began filling them with His Spirit. The effects of God's Spirit were similar in both situations.

People were so touched and emotionally moved that they were physically powerless to control their bodies. At the first temple dedication, the priests were unable to stand or minister because the presence of the Lord was so strong; at the feast of Pentecost, we see that people were acting in a manner that would otherwise be attributable to intoxication! God's presence is powerful and moving, and He wants to move for everyone! An invitation to God is not like inviting someone to a formal dinner party; it requires a decision to change your life. It is not a flippant request, but one that is born out of conviction, prayer, and reflective thought. We must take a hard look at our lives without God, recognize a need for change, and follow the decision with action. A decision without action is not a decision; it is only flirting with or contemplating a decision. Real decision requires action, and, in this instance, it requires repentance, a resolve to avoid sin, baptism in the name of Jesus Christ, and a request for the Holy Spirit to fill your temple.

> For if you live according to the flesh you
> will die; but if by the Spirit you put to
> death the deeds of the body, you will live.
> For as many as are led by the Spirit of God,
> these are sons of God. For you did not
> receive the spirit of bondage again to fear,
> but you received the Spirit of adoption by
> whom we cry out, Abba, Father. The Spirit
> Himself bears witness with our spirit that
> we are children of God, and if children,
> then heirs—heirs of God and joint heirs
> with Christ, if indeed we suffer with Him,
> that we may also be glorified together.
> (Romans 8:13-17, NKJV)

Paul tells us, "If by the Spirit you put to death the deeds of the body, you will live. For as many as are led by the Spirit of God, these are sons of God...you received the Spirit of adoption by whom we cry out...Father" (Romans 8:13-15, NKJV). In order to be adopted and have the benefits that come along with being an heir, we must first receive the Spirit of God! As we discussed, we must clean out our hearts, die to flesh through repentance, bury our sins in water baptism, and ask God to fill us with His own Holy Spirit! Without the Holy Spirit, we do not have His name; however, with the Holy Spirit comes eternal assurance! We do not have to wonder whether or not God filled our temple! God made it evident to Solomon and the Israelites; He also gives us evidence of His residence by using our tongue to herald His entrance! We are baptized in water in the name of Jesus because it is His name that commutes our sentence of death, but we are baptized in Spirit into the name of Jesus! Notice the difference between *in* and *into*. Water baptism is in the name of Jesus, but Spirit baptism is into the name of Jesus! When the Spirit of God takes up residence in our temple, our surname is changed through the process of adoption! When we are formed in our mother's womb, we do not have the Spirit of God. Christ had the Holy Spirit living inside of Him from the point He was created in the womb, but that is not true for us. Jesus inherited His name from God in

263

the womb of Mary, but ours is the process of adoption into the name of Jesus!

Allowing the Helper to Help

> In the law it is written: With men of other tongues and other lips I will speak to this people; And yet, for all that, they will not hear Me, says the Lord. Therefore tongues are for a sign, not to those who believe but to unbelievers; but prophesying is not for unbelievers but for those who believe. (1 Corinthians 14:21-22, NKJV)

It is an awesome feeling to experience the infilling of the Holy Spirit! We need that initial experience, and we need many more afterwards! This leads us into our next discussion of what it means to allow the Holy Spirit to lead us into full truth. Being led into something means we leave one area and move in a new direction. In order to be led by the Holy Spirit, we must apply the Word of God to our lives as we receive new revelation. This means we diligently study the Bible and pray for God to reveal His Word to us! The Holy Spirit will answer our prayer, and teach us truth!

> All scripture is given by inspiration of God,
> and is profitable for doctrine, for reproof,
> for correction, for instruction in
> righteousness: That the man of God may
> be perfect, thoroughly furnished unto all
> good works. (2 Timothy 3:16-17, KJV)

We should seek to interact with God as frequently as possible! We should set aside time to pray and study His Word every day. Our thoughts, conversations, and actions should be governed by His Words. It is not enough for us to have an experience with God; we must have daily experiences with Him. We need many of those experiences in order to help us avoid carnality, bolster Godly conviction, and embrace a walk with Christ. We, as humans, are blind and cannot know the ways of God unless we are led into them. The more time we spend with God, the more we are influenced by Him. The ultimate goal is to completely replace our old nature with the nature of Christ!

> But as it is written: Eye has not seen, nor
> ear heard, Nor have entered into the heart
> of man The things which God has prepared
> for those who love Him. But God has
> revealed them to us through His Spirit. For

the Spirit searches all things, yes, the deep things of God. For what man knows the things of a man except the spirit of the man which is in him? Even so no one knows the things of God except the Spirit of God. Now we have received, not the spirit of the world, but the Spirit who is from God, that we might know the things that have been freely given to us by God. (1 Corinthians 2:9-12, NKJV)

Then Jesus said to them again, Most assuredly, I say to you, I am the door of the sheep. All who ever came before Me are thieves and robbers, but the sheep did not hear them. I am the door. If anyone enters by Me, he will be saved, and will go in and out and find pasture. (John 10:7-9, NKJV)

For He says: In an acceptable time I have heard you, And in the day of salvation I have helped you. Behold, now is the accepted time; behold, now is the day of salvation. (2 Corinthians 6:2, NKJV)

Our ways are not His ways; therefore, we should not search for His ways through earthly knowledge. If our lives do not line up with the Holy Bible, we are not being led by the Spirit. Paul informs us, "That we might know the things that have been freely given to us by God" (1 Corinthians 2:12, NKJV). We enjoy free access to a merciful God! Before Jesus Christ died on the cross, mankind did not have free access to God. There were always rules and processes to follow in order to get in the mere proximity of God! However, today we can receive the Spirit of God, which gives us knowledge of the free blessings of God! Without His Spirit, we are oblivious to so many free gifts that are simply waiting for us to receive them! It is like a stubborn child that refuses to pause his play long enough to go into his parent's home. He does not realize he has gifts, desserts, and friends waiting just inside to throw him a surprise party! Since he cannot see the full picture, he thinks he is better off outside. This is exactly what many adults do; people often decide being outside of the Father's house is more beneficial than residing inside His house.

People search everywhere, but never truly find anything that fulfills their inner longings. They could experience unconditional love, fulfillment, true joy, inner peace, emotional gratification, and satisfaction. If only he or she could realize family and friends have been longing, praying, and believing for them to enter *The Door* of the Father's house. Jesus said, "I am the door. If anyone enters by Me, he will be saved" (John 10:9, NKJV). If you have not invited Jesus Christ to live and reside in your vessel, which is the only remaining temple of the living God, today is your day! Paul stressed that we should not delay when he said, "Now is the day of salvation" (2 Corinthians 6:2, NKJV). Today is the day to act because who knows what tomorrow holds!

> On the last day, that great day of the feast, Jesus stood and cried out, saying, If anyone thirsts, let him come to Me and drink. He who believes in Me, as the Scripture has said, out of his heart will flow rivers of living water. But this He spoke concerning the Spirit, whom those believing in Him would receive; for the Holy Spirit was not yet given, because Jesus was not yet glorified. (John 7:37-39, NKJV)

> But the fruit of the Spirit is love, joy, peace, longsuffering, kindness, goodness, faithfulness, gentleness, self-control. Against such there is no law. And those who are Christ's have crucified the flesh with its passions and desires. If we live in

the Spirit, let us also walk in the Spirit.
(Galatians 5:22-25, NKJV)

When the Holy Spirit resides inside of us, it is like a river of living water flowing inside of us! However, it will not stay inside of our body; the water will overflow once it has reached capacity! Everything we do, say, or even think will be influenced by this water! Everything the water touches will be transformed into life! Negative or perverse thoughts receive life! Our speech receives life! Our actions are full of life! It is like a new garden in the spring; the old dirt is turned over and out of it grows beneficial produce! Paul called this phenomenon, "The fruit of the Spirit" (Galatians 5:22, NKJV). Once we are filled with the Spirit of God, we begin to display love, joy, peace, patience, kindness, goodness, faithfulness, gentleness, and self-control! Who does not want a life altering experience that changes us into better people? I cannot think of a reason why anyone would willingly choose themselves over the person they could be in Christ!

O wretched man that I am! Who will
deliver me from this body of death?
(Romans 7:24, NKJV)

The heart is deceitful above all things, And
desperately wicked; Who can know it?
(Jeremiah 17:9, NKJV)

And even as they did not like to retain God
in their knowledge, God gave them over to
a debased mind, to do those things which
are not fitting. (Romans 1:28, NKJV)

Speaking lies in hypocrisy, having their own
conscience seared with a hot iron. (1
Timothy 4:2, NKJV)

Paul and Jeremiah both recognized the wicked nature into
which we are born. If you take a moment and contemplate the
state of our world, the wisdom of Paul and Jeremiah begins to
become vibrantly clear. How can someone commit murder,
abuse a child, or neglect someone that is helpless? All humans
are capable of wickedness because sin is corrosive. This is why
Jeremiah warns us that we should never wander into the
depths of our wicked heart. He says who can even know the
depth of our heart's wickedness? As we sin, we become
increasingly desensitized to sin and eventually completely
numb to it. Paul referred to this numb state as a "debased
mind" and having a "conscience seared with a hot iron"

(Romans 1:28; 1 Timothy 4:2, NKJV). I seriously doubt that anyone comes up with a five or ten year plan that includes addiction, physical abuse, anxiety, fear, or neglect. If no one is planning to include these things in their lives, why do so many people fall prey to them? It is because we cannot trust the desires of our fallen nature; our hearts are deceitful. We will seek after wealth, status, pleasure, and fame, but we will only find destruction. All roads do not lead to heaven; the only way to arrive at a destination of everlasting life is to follow the path provided by Jesus! The good news of Jesus Christ; as discussed in chapter three, He is the way, the truth, and the life.

We invite Christ into our lives by following the example offered by the disciples and early church and by seeking after the Holy Spirit through prayer, fasting, and study of God's word. Once the Holy Spirit enters into our bodies, it is critical that we be led into full truth by obeying and applying the Word to our lives on a daily basis! If we apply the Word of God daily and walk in its truth, we will be known as saints of the most High! Only then will we be able to partake in the victory of Jesus Christ!

SEVEN

The Fulfillment of Jesus Christ

Eternal Jesus

In this book, we have primarily focused on the reason and purpose for which Jesus, the Son of man, was created. In order to fully know Jesus, there are two additional eras of time that should be explored. There was a large span of time that transpired before Jesus was born to Mary, and there will be eons of time that will transpire after Jesus fulfills the purpose for which He was created. In this chapter, we will refer to these two eras as: 1) the pre-mortal era; and, 2) the post-victorious era. We will discuss how God manifested Himself during these two eras of time. We will define the pre-mortal era as the span of time before creation that ends with the birth of Jesus Christ. We will define the post-victorious era as the span of time after Jesus has defeated Satan and has judged all of mankind at the final white throne judgement. We are using expressions of time very loosely here because the Bible foretells of a physical existence of God's creation that continues after time comes to an end. In fact, the term *era* is misleading because it insinuates that there will be an end to this existence; however, that is not the case. The Bible refers to this final era as a period of "eternal life"; a perpetual existence with no end (1 John 2:25, NKJV).

> And this is the promise that He has promised us—eternal life. (1 John 2:25, NKJV)

> Before the mountains were brought forth, or ever thou hadst formed the earth and the world, even from everlasting to everlasting, thou art God. (Psalm 90:2, KJV)

> And behold, you will conceive in your womb and bring forth a Son, and shall call His name Jesus. He will be great, and will be called the Son of the Highest; and the Lord God will give Him the throne of His father David. And He will reign over the house of Jacob forever, and of His kingdom there will be no end. (Luke 1:31-33, NKJV)

For he who sows to his flesh will of the
flesh reap corruption, but he who sows to
the Spirit will of the Spirit reap everlasting
life. (Galatians 6:8, NKJV)

Psalms records that God is from everlasting to everlasting;
therefore, it is reasonable for us to refrain from limiting our
conversation about God by the insignificance of time. Rather,
we should discuss any manifestation of God that previously
existed or will exist during the spans of eternity we
parameterized in the first paragraph of this chapter. God
existed before time, matter, and space were ever created,
which is unfathomable to our finite minds; however, it is true. I
will not attempt to explain the origin of God, since He has no
beginning; however, I would like to discuss the origin of God's
manifestations. In this book, we have been using the term
manifestations, but if that term does not resonate with you,
you can simply interchange it with God's physical expression,
form, material state, or image. Regardless of the term you use,
at a point that predates creation, God decided He wanted a
physical manifestation to express His Spirit.

First, let us talk about Jesus before He was born to Mary
during the time we are calling *the pre-mortal era*. People often
discuss many things about Jesus including: (a) His birth, life,

and death while He was in His mortal body here on earth, (b) after His ascension into heaven, and (c) His millennial reign here on earth. One area that is often overlooked is the span of time that existed before He was born in the manger in Bethlehem. There are many verses that indicate God utilized physical manifestations well before Jesus was born as the Son of man! We will not discuss a comprehensive list; rather, we will simply review examples as evidence supporting the proof of pre-mortal manifestations.

> And to the angel of the church of the Laodiceans write, These things says the Amen, the Faithful and True Witness, the Beginning of the creation of God. (Revelation 3:14, NKJV)

> He is the image of the invisible God, the firstborn over all creation. For by Him all things were created that are in heaven and that are on earth, visible and invisible, whether thrones or dominions or principalities or powers. All things were created through Him and for Him. And He is before all things, and in Him all things consist. And He is the head of the body,

the church, who is the beginning, the firstborn from the dead, that in all things He may have the preeminence. (Colossians 1:15-17, NKJV)

In the beginning was the Word, and the Word was with God, and the Word was God. He was in the beginning with God. All things were made through Him, and without Him nothing was made that was made. In Him was life, and the life was the light of men. And the light shines in the darkness, and the darkness did not comprehend it. (John 1:1-5, NKJV)

And without controversy great is the mystery of godliness: God was manifested in the flesh, Justified in the Spirit, Seen by angels, Preached among the Gentiles, Believed on in the world, Received up in glory. (1 Timothy 3:16, NKJV)

So they rose up that very hour and returned to Jerusalem, and found the eleven and those who were with them gathered together, saying, The Lord is risen indeed, and has appeared to Simon! And

they told about the things that had
happened on the road, and how He was
known to them in the breaking of bread.
Now as they said these things, Jesus
Himself stood in the midst of them, and
said to them, Peace to you. But they were
terrified and frightened, and supposed
they had seen a spirit. (Luke 24:33-37,
NKJV)

But one testified in a certain place, saying:
What is man that You are mindful of him,
Or the son of man that You take care of
him? You have made him a little lower
than the angels; You have crowned him
with glory and honor, And set him over the
works of Your hands. You have put all
things in subjection under his feet.
(Hebrews 2:6-8, NKJV)

In chapter one, we reviewed a verse where God manifested
Himself to humans through the body of Jesus. We will discuss
this verse once again because it gives another vital clue that is
applicable here; this verse mentions the phrase, "seen of
angels" (1 Timothy 3:16, NKJV). This phrase is significant
because it tells us that, similar to humans, a spirit cannot be

seen by angels. If angels cannot see a spirit then God is invisible to angels unless He utilizes some manifestation to express His Spirit. With few exceptions, angels are invisible to humans, and, as we just learned, the Spirit of God is invisible to angels. This suggests there is a tiered system in God's creation. This tiered system of creation is supported by the writer of Hebrews, which states that humans were created a little lower than the angels (Hebrews 2:6-8, NKJV). Just like humans, angels are created beings. As we learned in chapter one, all of God's creation exists inside of Him; He is larger than His creation. Angels require a visible, albeit heavenly, physical form in order to see their Creator. It is equally plausible for God to create a heavenly body, which He used to communicate with His angels, just as He created an earthly body in order to communicate with mankind.

We are able to see the difference between the parallel earthly and heavenly physical realities when Jesus encountered His disciples after His resurrection (Luke 24:33-37, NKJV). The disciples were gathered talking about Jesus when He miraculously appeared in the midst of them! It was so startlingly unnatural that the disciples were terrified and afraid! Jesus went from being invisible to humans to being visible in the matter of an instant. Did Jesus' invisibility mean that He existed, ceased to exist, and then existed once again?

No, it means that He existed in an angelic, physical state that could not be seen by humans, and, when necessary, He made Himself visible in a humanly, physical state! Just as Christ did not cease to exist, He also did not change from an immortal human into a spirit and then back into an immortal human. Christ was and still is an immortal human!

I had not considered a pre-mortal existence of Jesus until one day when I was engaged in a conversation with a friend, and he called my attention to this topic. It was this conversation that first piqued my interest and made me seriously consider the existence of Jesus prior to His birth to Mary. I would like to call your attention back to the fact that God's name is Jesus, and He can use whatever manifestation He chooses! Do not lose sight that God is a single infinite, all powerful, all knowing, omnipresent, and invisible Spirit. As the Almighty God, He has the right to appear in the form of wind, water, light, shade, stone, trees, mammals, amphibians, or any other part of His creation!

With this concept in mind, let us analyze the remaining verses we listed previously in this chapter. It is clear that God used a physical being to create heaven, earth, and everything in the earth! The noun in Colossians 1:15 is an image, or physical form, of the invisible God (Colossians 1:15, NKJV). "Image" in this verse comes from a Greek word that means: An image, a statue, or representation (Strong, Eikon Meaning in Bible - New Testament Greek Lexicon - King James Version 1890). Paul says this image, or physical manifestation of God, was used to create all things! John says the physical manifestation of God was the first of God's creation, which is logical since God utilized this manifestation to create every subsequent creation (Revelation 3:14, NKJV). According to Reverend Todd Rosel, this physical manifestation is the same Logos as described by John. John spells it out clearly when he says, "In the beginning was the Word...All things were made through Him, and without Him nothing was made that was made" (John 1:1-3, NKJV). In this verse, "word" comes from a Greek word that does not have an English equivalent. The Greek word is transliterated into our alphabet as: "Logos" (Strong, Logos Meaning in Bible - New Testament Greek Lexicon - King James Version 1890). Logos is a Greek word that was used when trying to appeal to logical reason; however, Logos is not just a style of writing or speech. Instead, it "refers to the structure and content of the text itself" (Purdue Writing Lab, n.d.). In ancient Greece, Logos was logical because it contained the actual evidence or proof within its content! For example, I could tell you that I am currently thirty-six years of age because my date of birth is December 20, 1983 and today's date is June 10, 2020. I could also tell you a gym has three hundred members and provide a list of their names. Both of these scenarios exemplify a logos style of writing. In each scenario, you are able to see or hear the evidence and arrive at a logical conclusion. Logos is persuasive as a result of the proof that is heard or seen! Notice that this logical writing is not conceptual or theoretical; instead, it contains tangible proof within its content! John says, "All things were made through" this tangible Logos (John 1:3, NKJV). Therefore, a physical manifestation of God existed before all creation because it was used to create all things! We will also analyze a derivative of Logos that is found in the English language.

Logo is an English word that is derived from the Greek logos (Merriam-Webster, n.d.). We should all be knowledgeable of logo as a term because in western societies we are inundated with corporate branding! Most organizations design a logo in order to represent their brand to the public. When we think of Starbucks, many people will immediately see the image of the green mermaid in their mind's eye! A logo is a physical representation that is used to identify an entity or business. When you see an Exxon sign you reasonably expect that you will be able to fill up the gas tank in your vehicle. You do not require a peer reviewed article that explains how an Exxon sign typically means gasoline is for sale! The logical proof is in the logo! This is very similar to the Logos of God! The Logos is a manifestation that represents God to His creation!

God has used many manifestations throughout the history of time. The Logos of God was the initial physical representation of His Spirit. It might surprise you to know that the Logos of God is still in existence today! John says that Jesus Christ will return to earth, but He will be known as "The Word [Logos] of God" (Revelation 19:13, KJV). In this verse, we see that Jesus Christ is completely synonymous with the Logos of God; they are the same person! Jesus Christ had a beginning when He was created in Mary's womb, but we just learned that a physical Jesus existed before Christ. How can this be possible? There is only one link between these two physical bodies; John inextricably ties the manifestation of Jesus Christ to the original Logos of God through the Spirit of God Almighty. All manifestations of God still represent only One God!

One manifestation six thousand years ago is no different than a manifestation today; the God of the manifestation has not changed! John points out that through a manifestation, which is the physical Logos, God's creation was rendered into effect. The Logos literally brought the creation into being. John is not talking about God's ability to reason, remember, or contemplate a future creation; he is talking about a physical being that was used by God as a tool of creation. This first physical creation, or the Logos, is the literal catalyst God used to initialize and orchestrate time, space, and matter into existence. The Spirit of God obviously has the power to create because He created the Logos, but He chooses to use a physical being through which He wields His power! Remember, John tells us that nothing was made except through the physical Logos!

> So God created man in his own image, in the image of God created he him; male and female created he them. And God blessed them, and God said unto them, Be fruitful, and multiply, and replenish the earth, and subdue it: and have dominion over the fish of the sea, and over the fowl of the air, and over every living thing that moveth upon the earth. And God said, Behold, I have given you every herb bearing seed, which is upon the face of all the earth, and every tree, in the which is the fruit of a tree yielding seed; to you it shall be for meat. And to every beast of the earth, and to every fowl of the air, and to every thing that creepeth upon the earth, wherein there is life, I have given every green herb

for meat: and it was so. (Genesis 1:27-30, KJV)

And the Lord God formed man of the dust of the ground, and breathed into his nostrils the breath of life; and man became a living soul. (Genesis 2:7, KJV)

And the Scripture was fulfilled which says, Abraham believed God, and it was accounted to him for righteousness. And he was called the friend of God. (James 2:23, NKJV)

Through the initial manifestation of the Logos, God created everything, and, out of all creation, His most beloved are human beings. Why does God love humans so much? What makes humans stand apart from all other creation? The reason humans are preferred above all of creation is because God desires relationship, which is why He created us from the very beginning. God wants our companionship; the rest of creation is for our benefit, but we are for His benefit! Moses tells us that God created everything prior to creating humans, and God told mankind to "have dominion over the fish of the sea, and over the fowl of the air, and over every living thing that moveth upon the earth" (Genesis 1:28, KJV). Mankind was not just another part of God's creation; we are the reason why everything else was created! We needed an environment, so God created this wonderful world as our habitat. We also see that mankind was created in the image of God! We do not read that any other part of creation was created to look like God! God spoke all of creation into existence except for humans. God formed man as if He were a potter molding clay!

We have already established that God does not have a face or hands, so what does it mean for humans to be created in the image of God? God first created for Himself a physical body, and then He created all mankind following a similar design. The Logos of God was the initial pattern God used to create all of mankind. When we look back over what we know of the history of the world, God's plan makes perfect sense! God desired relationship, so He created a body for Himself, and He created other bodies with which to interact! However, to have true relationship, each body must willingly choose to enter into relationship with Him. God accomplished this by creating a vast environment called Earth where humans can learn about God and choose for themselves whether or not to love Him. To complete the process, God became an official part of creation by entering into man's environment through Jesus Christ.

It was through Jesus Christ that God was finally able to establish the relationship for which He desired from the very beginning! It is the man Jesus Christ that brings fulfillment to the plan of God! James informs us that, due to Abraham's relationship with God, he was given a title, "The Friend of God" (James 2:23, NKJV). We should all be eagerly awaiting the return of Jesus Christ because this is God's plan of relationship! The plan is this: For humanity to willingly choose Jesus, and, through this choice, become friends of Almighty God.

> There is no fear in love; but perfect love casts out fear, because fear involves torment. But he who fears has not been made perfect in love. We love Him because He first loved us. (1 John 4:18-19, NKJV)

> He who has My commandments and keeps them, it is he who loves Me. And he who loves Me will be loved by My Father, and I will love him and manifest Myself to him. (John 14:21, NKJV)

John provides a summary of why God created the earth as our habitat and why He created us for relationship (1 John 4:19, NKJV). It simply says, "Because he first loved us." This is not only talking about Christ suffering and dying on the cross for our sins; it goes back to the moment breath was breathed into the nostrils of mankind! God gave us a body that looks like His body, and He breathed life into us. He gave us a mind, which enabled free will, so we can learn about Him and His love! John tells us that our confidence is built upon our love of God! In other words, we can trust in Him because He loves us; therefore, we have nothing to fear (1 John 4:18-19, NKJV). Fear comes when doubt enters into our minds. If we doubt that God loves us, cares for us, can change us, or will forgive us then we have fear, torment, and condemnation. Jesus clues us into the solution of how we can ensure that we abide in God's love. He says to keep His commandments because that is how we return love to God! Relationship is built on a two-way street of love! We enter into relationship with God when we love Him through obedience! Jesus said He will manifest Himself through the Holy Spirit, if we simply obey His commandments (John 14:21, NKJV). We cannot pick and choose which commandments to follow; it is all or nothing! Believing truth is obeying truth, which is why those that believe will be saved, and being saved is simply entering into a relationship with Jesus Christ!

The fact that a physical Jesus created everything before being born to Mary is not at all detrimental to the Hebrew

Shema. In case you have forgotten about the Hebrew Shema, we discussed it in chapter two; Moses penned the words of God to His people (Deuteronomy 6:4-9, NKJV). It is the foundation of the Hebrew belief in God, and it definitively states that God is a singular entity; He is only one Lord. Let me explain why a Jesus that predates a birth to Mary does not contradict the Hebrew Shema. God existed before creation, so any created thing is inferior, and, therefore, under the authority of its original source. God manifested Himself in a heavenly body in order to communicate with angels; similarly, God manifested Himself in an earthly body in order to communicate with humans. God is God, which inherently gives Him the authority and ability to do as He pleases. As an all-powerful being, God can do whatever He wants; and, according to His scripture, He utilized a physical form in the heavens before Christ was born here on earth.

> And the angel of the Lord found her by a
> fountain of water in the wilderness, by the
> fountain in the way to Shur. (Genesis 16:7,
> KJV)

Occasionally the Bible will reference the *angel of the Lord*. Often in these cases, Angel is translated from a Hebrew word meaning: a messenger (Strong, Mal'ak Meaning in Bible - Old Testament Hebrew Lexicon - King James Version 1890). Many times it refers to an angel sent on an errand by God, but occasionally it appears to refer to a physical representation, or manifestation, of God.

> And the Angel of the Lord said to Manoah, Though you detain Me, I will not eat your food. But if you offer a burnt offering, you must offer it to the Lord. (For Manoah did not know He was the Angel of the Lord). (Judges 13:16, NKJV)

> Now the Angel of the Lord came and sat under the terebinth tree which was in Ophrah, which belonged to Joash the Abiezrite, while his son Gideon threshed wheat in the winepress, in order to hide it from the Midianites. And the Angel of the Lord appeared to him, and said to him, The Lord is with you, you mighty man of valor! Gideon said to Him, O my lord, if the Lord is with us, why then has all this happened to us? And where are all His miracles which our fathers told us about, saying, Did not the Lord bring us up from Egypt? But now

the Lord has forsaken us and delivered us into the hands of the Midianites. Then the Lord turned to him and said, Go in this might of yours, and you shall save Israel from the hand of the Midianites. Have I not sent you? So he said to Him, O my Lord, how can I save Israel? Indeed my clan is the weakest in Manasseh, and I am the least in my father's house. And the Lord said to him, Surely I will be with you, and you shall defeat the Midianites as one man. Then he said to Him, If now I have found favor in Your sight, then show me a sign that it is You who talk with me. Do not depart from here, I pray, until I come to You and bring out my offering and set it before You. And He said, I will wait until you come back. So Gideon went in and prepared a young goat, and unleavened bread from an ephah of flour. The meat he put in a basket, and he put the broth in a pot; and he brought them out to Him under the terebinth tree and presented them. The Angel of God said to him, Take the meat and the unleavened bread and lay them on this rock, and pour out the broth. And he did so. Then the

Angel of the Lord put out the end of the staff that was in His hand, and touched the meat and the unleavened bread; and fire rose out of the rock and consumed the meat and the unleavened bread. And the Angel of the Lord departed out of his sight. Now Gideon perceived that He was the Angel of the Lord. So Gideon said, Alas, O Lord God! For I have seen the Angel of the Lord face to face. Then the Lord said to him, Peace be with you; do not fear, you shall not die. (Judges 6:11-23, NKJV)

The angels in Judges 13 and Judges 6 act completely different when a sacrifice is presented to them. Notice that the angel in Judges 13 makes it clear that a sacrifice should not be offered to him by saying, "If you offer a burnt offering, you must offer it to the Lord" (Judges 13:16, NKJV). The Bible makes it clear that the angel in Judges 13 is just a messenger from God and not a manifestation of God. However, contrast the response of the angel in Judges 13 to the angel in Judges 6. In Judges 6, the angel waits for Gideon to prepare a sacrifice and then participates in the sacrifice (Judges 6:17-21, NKJV). Judges 6 refers to the angel when it says, "The Lord turned to him and said, 'Go in this might of yours, and you shall save

Israel from the hand of the Midianites'" (Judges 6:14, NKJV). Gideon even refers to this angel as "Lord God" (Judges 6:22, NKJV). It seems plausible that the angel Gideon met in Judges 6 was actually a manifestation of God!

> And the angel of the Lord appeared unto him in a flame of fire out of the midst of a bush: and he looked, and, behold, the bush burned with fire, and the bush was not consumed. And Moses said, I will now turn aside, and see this great sight, why the bush is not burnt. And when the Lord saw that he turned aside to see, God called unto him out of the midst of the bush, and said, Moses, Moses. And he said, Here am I. And he said, Draw not nigh hither: put off thy shoes from off thy feet, for the place whereon thou standest is holy ground. Moreover he said, I am the God of thy father, the God of Abraham, the God of Isaac, and the God of Jacob. And Moses hid his face; for he was afraid to look upon God. (Exodus 3:2-6, KJV)

The angel in Exodus 3 referred to Himself as "the God of Abraham, the God of Isaac, and the God of Jacob" (Exodus 3:6,

KJV). This angel of God was more like the angel in Judges 6, which had more authority than the angel in Judges 13. This angel told Moses to take off his shoes because he was standing on holy ground. Ground can only be holy if it is made holy by The Holy One! The ground was holy because Moses stood in the presence of Almighty God!

> Then King Nebuchadnezzar was astonished; and he rose in haste and spoke, saying to his counselors, Did we not cast three men bound into the midst of the fire? They answered and said to the king, True, O king. Look! he answered, I see four men loose, walking in the midst of the fire; and they are not hurt, and the form of the fourth is like the Son of God. Then Nebuchadnezzar went near the mouth of the burning fiery furnace and spoke, saying, Shadrach, Meshach, and Abed-Nego, servants of the Most High God, come out, and come here. Then Shadrach, Meshach, and Abed-Nego came from the midst of the fire. (Daniel 3:24-26, NKJV)

The fourth man in the fire is such an exciting story of God! God came to the aid of three Hebrews that were standing against the ruler of the world! God could have stepped in at any point before these men were thrown into the fire. He could have sent a wind to knock over the statue, angels to kill the soldiers, or rain to drown out the fire; however, God chose to save them at their point of death! God made Himself visible in the form of a man without ever ceasing to be an omnipresent God! What kind of God can retain His Spiritual form and also exist in a physical state as well? The Almighty God has this power!

In the middle of Nebuchadnezzar's sweltering furnace, a human manifestation of God defied a heathen king and saved three men that refused to bow to a false idol. When Nebuchadnezzar awoke that morning, I am sure he planned to display his own greatness in front of his country's leaders, but he had to step aside as God manifested His glory for all to see! No one had any reason to leave Nebuchadnezzar's party wondering whether or not the Hebrew's God is supreme. God's power was clearly visible and blatantly evident! Can you imagine watching three men be bound, dragged, and thrown into a fire, but see them walk out unharmed? You would know that the fire was hot after seeing the guards die from the heat (Daniel 3:22, NKJV). It was hot enough to kill the guards, but not hot enough to kill God! The three Hebrew men were tied up when they went into the fire, but their ropes were the only things that burned!

The Babylonian king went from anger to awe in the presence of God. The day that started with worship to a golden idol, turned into worship of Almighty God! Nebuchadnezzar acknowledged God and recognized His deity in front of the entire audience. These people traveled from all areas of the kingdom in order to attend this statue dedication (Daniel 3:3, NKJV). However, they got a show that they would undoubtedly never forget.

We should also acknowledge God's power, and we should realize that He can utilize any physical form He chooses while maintaining His Spiritual characteristics. God does not change even when He takes the form of a man in the middle of a fiery furnace. Is there anything that God cannot do? Just like the people at the golden statue dedication, I am convinced God has no boundaries and there is no limit to His power. Our limits in understanding should never be projected upon God; He has proven time and again that He is more than able to accomplish any goal by any means He prefers.

> And the Lord said, Because the cry of
> Sodom and Gomorrah is great, and
> because their sin is very grievous; I will go

down now, and see whether they have
done altogether according to the cry of it,
which is come unto me; and if not, I will
know. And the men turned their faces from
thence, and went toward Sodom: but
Abraham stood yet before the Lord.
(Genesis 18:20-22, KJV)

There are other accounts of God manifesting Himself to
humans before the Messiah was born of Mary. One of the
more obvious accounts is when God, as a human man, shares a
meal with Abraham before going to destroy the wicked cities
of Sodom and Gomorrah (Genesis 18:20-22, KJV). God used a
physical body before the Messiah was born on many occasions
in both heaven and on earth. Multiple manifestations of God
do not alter the truth that God is the single, all-powerful,
almighty ruler of the universe! On the contrary, it proves that
He is all powerful because He can appear in any form He
chooses; every manifestation of God will still bear His name,
the name of Jesus.

For this Melchizedek, king of Salem, priest
of the Most High God, who met Abraham
returning from the slaughter of the kings
and blessed him, to whom also Abraham

gave a tenth part of all, first being
translated king of righteousness, and then
also king of Salem, meaning king of peace,
without father, without mother, without
genealogy, having neither beginning of
days nor end of life, but made like the Son
of God, remains a priest continually.
(Hebrews 7:1-3, NKJV)

The Lord said to my Lord, Sit at My right
hand, Till I make Your enemies Your
footstool. The Lord shall send the rod of
Your strength out of Zion. Rule in the midst
of Your enemies! Your people shall be
volunteers In the day of Your power; In the
beauties of holiness, from the womb of the
morning, You have the dew of Your youth.
The Lord has sworn And will not relent,
You are a priest forever According to the
order of Melchizedek. (Psalm 110:1-4,
NKJV)

For David did not ascend into the heavens,
but he says himself: The Lord said to my
Lord, Sit at My right hand, Till I make Your
enemies Your footstool. Therefore let all

the house of Israel know assuredly that God has made this Jesus, whom you crucified, both Lord and Christ. (Acts 2:34-36, NKJV)

According to Reverend Todd Rosel, Melchisedec could very well be another example of a human manifestation of God before Jesus' birth to Mary; He had no father, no mother, no beginning, and no ending. This sounds very much like a description of God! God had no beginning and will have no end! During Peter's first sermon, he draws a direct correlation between David's prophecy in Psalm 110 and Jesus Christ (Psalm 110:1-4; Acts 2:36, NKJV). David prophesied that a man, like Melchisedec, would be both Lord and Christ. Christ here is talking about the human; Lord here is talking about Almighty God. Peter ties up the loose ends by saying, "God has made this Jesus, whom you crucified, both Lord and Christ" (Acts 2:36, NKJV). Also, notice how David references, "According to the order of Melchizedek" (Psalm 110:4, NKJV). In this verse, "order" is translated from a Hebrew word that means: manner (Strong, Dibrah Meaning in Bible - Old Testament Hebrew Lexicon - King James Version 1890). Jesus Christ would be designed after the same manner, or pattern, of all previous manifestations. The pattern is this: The Spirit of God works through a physical vessel in order to accomplish His purpose. This is why David could prophesy that Jesus would be after the order of Melchisedec. The design was the same and their role to mankind was also similar.

> But Christ came as High Priest of the good things to come, with the greater and more perfect tabernacle not made with hands, that is, not of this creation. Not with the blood of goats and calves, but with His own blood He entered the Most Holy Place once for all, having obtained eternal redemption. For if the blood of bulls and goats and the ashes of a heifer, sprinkling the unclean, sanctifies for the purifying of the flesh, how much more shall the blood of Christ, who through the eternal Spirit offered Himself without spot to God, cleanse your conscience from dead works to serve the living God? And for this reason He is the Mediator of the new covenant, by means of death, for the redemption of the transgressions under the first covenant, that those who are called may receive the promise of the eternal inheritance. (Hebrews 9:11-15, NKJV)

Melchisedec was a priest unto God working on behalf of Abraham. It is not by accident that Abraham, the man who entered into covenant with God, required a mediator in order to help facilitate the gap between sin and salvation. Abraham was unable to accomplish this task alone! This foreshadowed the role that Jesus would fulfill for all of humanity today. Due to our sin, we are unable to access God except through the Mediator, our High Priest. The writer of Hebrews says, "Christ came as High Priest...with His own blood...who through the eternal Spirit offered Himself without spot to God...And for this reason He is the Mediator of the new covenant" (Hebrews 9:11-15, NKJV). Melchisedec was the mediator of the old testament between God and Abraham, and Jesus Christ has become the mediator of the new testament between God and all mankind! The order, or pattern, of Melchisedec is to be the mediator between sin and salvation!

> And I will put enmity between thee and the woman, and between thy seed and her seed; it shall bruise thy head, and thou shalt bruise his heel. (Genesis 3:15, KJV)

> The devil, who deceived them, was cast into the lake of fire and brimstone where the beast and the false prophet are. And

> they will be tormented day and night
> forever and ever. (Revelation 20:10, NKJV)

We have been discussing how God set a precedent of using manifestations, which is how Jesus existed before being born into this earth. In case it is not clear, I will sum it up before moving on from this point. God revealed His name approximately two thousand years ago, which is Jesus. God also used many manifestations prior to the human birth of Jesus Christ; therefore, Jesus truly has no origin because God has no origin. However, Jesus our God started using physical manifestations before creation, and we know this is true because He used a physical manifestation when He created all things.

> Then comes the end, when He delivers the kingdom to God the Father, when He puts an end to all rule and all authority and power. (1 Corinthians 15:24, NKJV)

> Now when all things are made subject to Him, then the Son Himself will also be subject to Him who put all things under Him, that God may be all in all. (1 Corinthians 15:28, NKJV)

Since we know that physical manifestations of God have an origin, let us shift our focus to what will happen to the physical manifestation of Jesus Christ once He fulfills the purpose for which He was created. We have dubbed this period as the *post-victorious era*. Paul answers this question when he speaks of "the end", which is the time after Jesus "puts an end to all rule and all authority and power" (1 Corinthians 15:24, NKJV). After Jesus' one thousand year reign on earth has ended, He will cast Satan into a place of eternal torment. The defeat of Satan will mark the fulfillment of Jesus Christ's purpose. Genesis 3 contains a prophecy that a human man would be born that would defeat Satan (Genesis 3:15, KJV). At this point in time, Satan will be permanently defeated, never to rise again. His existence will continue, since he is immortal, but he will be forever bound. The enemy of our souls will ultimately lose the battle and our savior will win!

Heaven

> Now I saw a new heaven and a new earth,
> for the first heaven and the first earth had
> passed away. Also there was no more sea.
> Then I, John, saw the holy city, New
> Jerusalem, coming down out of heaven
> from God, prepared as a bride adorned for

her husband. And I heard a loud voice from heaven saying, Behold, the tabernacle of God is with men, and He will dwell with them, and they shall be His people. God Himself will be with them and be their God. (Revelation 21:1-3, NKJV)

We will take this opportunity to explain the concept of heaven in order to provide context for the point in time at which Satan will be defeated. Most of us have heard about heaven during the course of our lives; there are many stories and songs about it. I am sure many have heard songs about streets of gold, mansions, or a glistening paradise. However, the heaven that everyone expects may not be the heaven that will actually exist! This type of environment is described in the Bible, but it does not mean what most people think! This may come as a surprise to many, but the Bible actually speaks about multiple earths and multiple heavens. In fact, there are two earths and three distinct heavens referenced throughout the pages of scripture. When you take a close look at the Bible, many stories and preconceptions of heaven may be debunked!

The first earth is obviously the planet on which we stand today; the first heaven is just as easy to identify, it is the outer space which surrounds the earth (Genesis 1:17-18, KJV). Since we are intimately familiar with the first heaven and earth set, we can assume no additional detail is required to explain them. Even though there is an odd number of earths and heavens, there are only two points in time at which all of this transition occurs; therefore, we will refer to them in sets of two because the earth and heaven always transition simultaneously. It should not surprise you that the two transition points are marked by two very significant events in the Bible! In order to ensure that we are all on the same page, the transitions will occur as follows: the first heaven and earth will be replaced by the second heaven and earth, which will then be replaced by the third Heaven.

The second set of heaven and earth will be very similar to the first. In fact, much of the rock, dirt, plants, animals, and people will remain from one earth to the next; the Bible is not quite as clear about what will happen in outer space, but it is likely that it will retain many of the same characteristics as well. However, the Bible is clear that there will be a major physical change to earth; we are told that extreme heat will accompany Christ's returns, which will burn up the first heaven and earth (2 Peter 3:10, KJV). Peter goes on to tell us that a righteous heaven and earth will replace the first set of heaven and earth. We know that the heat will not exterminate the earth's population; therefore, the heat must be isolated to portions of the earth or a subset of mortal people will be protected from it. We know this is true because people that are alive before the transition will remain alive afterwards; Christ and His saints will rule over these people on the new earth for one thousand years after His return (Baxter, 2015). Since people continue to live into Christ's millennial Kingdom, we know that the earth does not explode or literally melt at this first transition. However, it appears that there will be a significant heat that is powerful enough to evaporate the water into the atmosphere around earth (Revelation 21:1, NKJV).

When the earth was created, God placed a layer of water around the earth to protect the inhabitants from ultraviolet light (Genesis 1:6-9, KJV). This protective layer of water existed around the earth until Noah was six hundred years old; at that time the water fell and flooded the earth (Genesis 7:6, KJV). After the protective layer of water fell, the life expectancy of men and women was greatly reduced (Genesis 6:3, KJV). It appears that this process will be reversed when Christ returns; water will once again form a protective layer around the earth for one thousand years. This protective layer will likely be the catalyst that helps extend the lives of mortal humans during the millennial reign of Christ (Daniel 7:12, NKJV). The earth was cursed because of sin, and, since that time, it has become increasingly tumultuous (Genesis 3:17; 5:29, KJV). We see this turmoil through the rise in natural disasters, cataclysmic events, and pandemics; however, this will one day be reversed! The whole earth will be full of God's glory (Isaiah 6:3, KJV). His glory began to fill the earth when Jesus poured His Spirit out on mankind, but it will be made complete once He begins to physically dwell on earth as our King!

The second heaven and earth will not only physically look different; they will be spiritually new as well! This old heaven and earth will be made new by having a new King! When Christ returns, human government will be dissolved; Christ alone will rule the world. Unfettered righteousness will burn up evil with a veracious heat. Wickedness will literally be consumed by the fire of God! We know the environment on earth will be free from violence, sorrow, suffering, or any resemblance of former wickedness; the world will move from the darkness we experience now to spiritual light (Revelation 21:4, KJV). There will be complete and unhindered peace on earth during Christ's earthly Kingdom (Isaiah 65:17-25, KJV). At this point, the heavens will also be made new; there will be peace in heaven since Christ's angelic enemies will be bound for one thousand years (Revelation 20:1-3, NKJV). The first heaven and earth transition is physical and spiritual, and the burning heat is both literal and metaphorical. It is literal because the earth will be physically overhauled by Christ, and it is metaphorical because it explains the spiritual difference between how the world is ruled today versus how it will be ruled during Christ's Kingdom!

We will now move momentarily from the literal to the figurative. During the first transition, the Bible prophesies that something will descend from heaven along with Christ when He returns to earth (Revelation 21:2, NKJV). In this verse, John refers to this mass as a city, which he calls "New Jerusalem"; he says this city will descend from heaven and exist here on earth during Christ's earthly Kingdom. The modern perception of heaven is derived from John's description of New Jerusalem. John tells us that the city's walls will be jasper, the city itself will consist of translucent gold, the twelve foundations of the city will be constructed of precious stone, and the gates will be made of pearl (Revelation 21:18-21, NKJV). When people get a mental image of heaven, this passage is likely the source of that image because John paints a magnificent picture of this city!

We learned earlier that one furlong is approximately a tenth of a mile (Endtime Magazine Articles, 2010). We can interpret John's specifications in order to understand the sheer grandeur of this city: one thousand and two hundred miles wide, one thousand and two hundred miles long, and one thousand and two hundred miles tall (Revelation 21:16, NKJV). To put this into context, New Jerusalem will cover an area that is slightly larger than Greenland (Central Intelligence Agency, 2018). The question we have to answer is this: Will an actual city descend with Christ or is John describing something altogether different? It seems unlikely that a physical city will fall to earth from somewhere in outer space. With any force at all, a mass the size of Greenland could quickly annihilate the earth! We know there will be an earthquake when Jesus touches down, but it will be caused by Jesus, not a comet-city (Zechariah 14:4-5, NKJV). If John is speaking figuratively, what could this city represent?

There are several clues we should consider when seeking to understand this city; these clues help us decipher the reality of John's prophecy. John tells us that the city comes down from heaven like a bride ready to marry her husband (Revelation 21:2, NKJV). We also see that the only inhabitants of New Jerusalem are the people documented in the Lamb's Book of Life (Revelation 21:27, NKJV). The biggest clue is when one of the seven angels reveals to John the bride of the Lamb, which turns out to be the New Jerusalem (Revelation 21:9-10, NKJV). We also get a clue by looking at who will accompany Jesus when He returns to earth; Zechariah tells us it is His saints (Zechariah 14:5, NKJV).

If the city is a collection of people, why give the size of the city? For a moment try to image how many people have been born and died since the dawn of creation. Is it possible that John is describing a huge crowd of people following after Christ? If you consider all references of Christ's return, this appears to be exactly what John is describing! If the content of the city is gold, why is this metaphor used to describe the people of God? The answer is explained by Zechariah, the saints of God will be tried as gold, and they will be found pure (Zechariah 13:8-9, KJV). The pure gold of New Jerusalem is the righteousness of God! People will no longer retain their identity; they will be identified by their resemblance to God! Just like Abraham searched for a city built by God; the people that find this city will be those who searched for it during their lives on earth (Hebrews 11:10, NKJV).

The picture John paints for us is that of Jesus Christ when He descends from heaven at the seventh trumpet; it is a description of when He leads His saints to the Battle of Armageddon. New Jerusalem is the bride of Christ, which will be the saints He gathers just prior to His descent! You might ask: Why is the bride of Christ called the New Jerusalem? As we discussed earlier in this book, Jerusalem is the place God chose to inhabit when He filled Solomon's Temple. Isaiah tells us that God will recreate Jerusalem and will joy in His people;

this recreated Jerusalem will be a group of people, not a city or building (Isaiah 65:17-19, KJV). God no longer inhabits a building located in Israel; instead, He inhabits people! The Old Testament relationship God had with the Jews has been replaced with a New Testament relationship with all people. Testament simply means an agreement, so the New Testament of the Bible covers the new agreement with all mankind! The people of the New Testament, which are filled with the Holy Spirit, are His New Jerusalem! We are the new temple of God!

The second transition will occur after Christ's one thousand year reign. At the end of Christ's Kingdom, Satan will lead a revolt against Him, which will end disastrously for Christ's opposition (Revelation 20:7-9, NKJV). God will devour Satan's army with fire, which brings with it the second transition of worlds. This second transition does not include an earth; it only affords a Heaven to its residents! This transition is marked by the judgment of all creation; Jesus will summons all dead and alive to appear before His throne (Revelation 20:11, NKJV). This verse tells us that people will flee from Christ's summons, but the second heaven and earth will no longer be found. The only place to run will be before Christ's throne, but this transition brings with it eternal judgement. Neither a hiding place nor mercy will be found; this will be the point at which there is no return. This is the most unfortunate event in all of history.

Tears have been wept by many over their loved ones because of this fateful day. Everyone should pray that the people they love will be prepared for this event. If we are caught ill-prepared, we will be forever separated from Christ. In chapter five, we learned that being separated from Christ means to exist in a place of eternal torment. This is a place we should avoid at all cost!

After the one thousand year earthly Kingdom of Christ, the physical earth will be abandoned. We will no longer inhabit this earth, but something much greater is in store! There is a third Heaven, which is a paradise that Paul was unable to describe (2 Corinthians 12:2-4, NKJV). This passage tells us that this paradise Heaven is so magnificent that humans are presently not allowed to hear or know about its wonders! It was to this paradise that one of the criminals went after dying on the cross beside Christ (Luke 23:43, KJV). This is also the primary residence for angels, and it is the place from which Satan and his angels will be banished in the years leading up to Christ's return (Revelation 12:7-10, KJV). In this passage, we see that this heaven is presently in existence because Satan and his angels visit this location in order to hurl accusations against Christians living on earth. This will continue until an angelic war occurs between Michael's army and Satan's army, which prompts Satan's expulsion from heaven. At this point, Satan will realize he is almost out of time and will intensify his efforts to damn all humanity; this period of time is synonymous with the Great Tribulation as described by Jesus (Matthew 24:16-21, NKJV). However, for Christians that overcome Satan, the reward will be wonderful! According to John, this Heaven is the final destination for the saints of God (Revelation 2:7, KJV).

The transition to the third Heaven is the point at which Satan will be defeated! Christ's return to earth will be the first transition, and His judgment is going to be the second transition (Revelation 20:10-15, NKJV). In this passage, we see that Christ's judgment is known as the second death, and it is at this point that all creation will be judged. Both angel and human will receive their just reward; those that are found faithful to Christ will enter into paradise, but those who chose disobedience will be banished to a lake of fire. We are told that to love Christ is to keep His commandments (2 John 1:6, KJV). This means that failing to keep His commandments equates to failing to love Him! Paul reminds us that crowns are prepared for everyone that "love" Christ's appearing (2 Timothy 4:8, KJV). Loving the appearance of Christ means that people anxiously anticipate Him; however, it also means that people are keeping His commandments until He returns! If we love Christ until He returns, we will transition with Christ from earth to eternal Paradise!

After Victory

> And behold, you will conceive in your
> womb and bring forth a Son, and shall call
> His name Jesus. He will be great, and will
> be called the Son of the Highest; and the
> Lord God will give Him the throne of His
> father David. And He will reign over the
> house of Jacob forever, and of His kingdom
> there will be no end. (Luke 1:31-33, NKJV)

Just like all other manifestations of God, Paul foretells of a time when the manifestation of Jesus Christ, the Son of man, will cease. To be clear, the abandonment of the body of Christ does not mean God will cease to exist! God did not cease to exist when His body disappeared following the walk in Nebuchadnezzar's fiery furnace! This is because the Spirit of God is eternal! Once Jesus returns to earth a second time, gathers His saints, reigns for one thousand years, judges all humanity, and, finally, casts Satan into the lake of fire, the transformed human body of Jesus will have fulfilled His purpose. At this point, Jesus will cease to manifest Himself through the human body of the Messiah, but, Jesus, the Almighty God, will continue unscathed into eternity!

This is the offering of Aaron and his sons,
which they shall offer to the Lord,
beginning on the day when he is anointed:
one-tenth of an ephah of fine flour as a
daily grain offering, half of it in the
morning and half of it at night. (Leviticus
6:20, NKJV)

I hope this question has been answered by now, but, if not, some may wonder: How the rule of Jesus can have no end while Jesus Christ will come to an end? The word Christ is the key here. In the Bible, Christ is translated from a Greek word that means: the anointed one; the Messiah (Strong, Christos Meaning in Bible - New Testament Greek Lexicon - King James Version 1890). When someone was anointed in the Old Testament it meant that person was commissioned to complete a specific job on God's behalf. Moses talked about Aaron and his sons' role as priests; they were anointed to fulfill a service to God (Leviticus 6:20, NKJV). There was a specific process that would cleanse a person for God's service; this process included pouring oil over the one being anointed.

Jesus Christ is the human manifestation that was anointed to fulfill the will of God. The Spirit of the Lord was the oil that was poured over Him before He was born into this earth. It was the Spirit that cleansed and helped Him accomplish His commission. Jesus Christ was tried by the fires of temptation, persecution, hardship, and betrayal; He was commissioned to reconcile mankind back to God and to defeat the enemies of God. We already know that part of the work Jesus Christ was commissioned to do has been fulfilled; we also know He will ultimately be successful! Once the job is finished and He is successful in completing His commission, the anointed manifestation will cease; however, Jesus will not! The commission will end, but the commissioner is eternal.

We can look back over the course of history and see that Jesus loves humanity more than anything else, so it is possible that He may choose to create a new manifestation in order to facilitate relationship with us. However, any speculation on what physical form God might take would simply be conjecture. The Bible does not offer a great deal of insight into how God might manifest Himself after the Messiah, but we do know that Jesus will continue to rule forever! The wardrobe of Jesus may change, but the God of the wardrobe will never change! He will continue to be the God that He has always been! His power will not cease, His knowledge will not fail, His presence will persist, and He will have no end!

And what agreement has the temple of
God with idols? For you are the temple of

the living God. As God has said: I will dwell in them And walk among them. I will be their God, And they shall be My people. (2 Corinthians 6:16, NKJV)

Let your conduct be without covetousness; be content with such things as you have. For He Himself has said, I will never leave you nor forsake you. So we may boldly say: The Lord is my helper; I will not fear. What can man do to me? (Hebrews 13:5, NKJV)

And I will pray the Father, and He will give you another Helper, that He may abide with you forever. (John 14:16, NKJV)

I know a man in Christ who fourteen years ago—whether in the body I do not know, or whether out of the body I do not know, God knows—such a one was caught up to the third heaven. And I know such a man— whether in the body or out of the body I do not know, God knows— how he was caught up into Paradise and heard inexpressible words, which it is not lawful for a man to utter. (2 Corinthians 12:2-4, NKJV)

Even though we do not know the future we can be certain that Jesus' promises will come to pass. Jesus will dwell in us, He will be our God, and we will be His people. He promised He will never leave us nor forsake us! Rest assured Jesus our God will never leave and He will never forsake because that is His promise! He may or may not take on a new form, but He will always be as close as a whisper. Jesus Christ said, "The Father...will give you another Helper, that He may abide with you forever" (John 14:16, NKJV). The Spirit of God will abide within us for all eternity! Whether or not we are able to see a physical Jesus, we can rely on the fact that we will live with Him forever! There is no need to have anxiety or fear of the future even though we do not know God's full plan; His promises are true and our story is certain to be exhilarating! We must ensure that we are included in the number of saints that have an opportunity to witness this story unfold! The eyes of the saints will behold this exciting promise one way or another. Wherever God chooses to lead us, it will be a fabulous journey! As we walk with Jesus, the incentives continue to grow and the distractions consistently diminish.

> Therefore I run thus: not with uncertainty.
> Thus I fight: not as one who beats the air.
> But I discipline my body and bring it into

subjection, lest, when I have preached to
others, I myself should become
disqualified. (1 Corinthians 9:26-27, NKJV)

Now when the seven thunders uttered
their voices, I was about to write; but I
heard a voice from heaven saying to me,
Seal up the things which the seven
thunders uttered, and do not write them.
(Revelation 10:4, NKJV)

The plan Jesus has for us is so magnificent and so fantastic
that we cannot truly fathom their grandeur. In fact, just as Paul
was not allowed to describe the Third Heaven, John the
Revelator was also not allowed to share with us the seven
thunders! The Word of God gives us great insight into what lies
ahead, but I believe what the future holds cannot be
adequately described on paper. If we were to speak with
someone who has passed from this life, I can just imagine he or
she would tell us, *you have to see it to believe it*! Paul says he
kept his body under subjection because he had his eyes on the
true goal. He did not want anything in this life to disqualify him
from the welcome party Jesus had waiting for him! We must
have the same attitude as Paul. Anything that distracts us in
this life should be cast aside, and our vision should be clearly

focused on our goal. Wherever our eyes gaze, that is the direction we will travel. If we are looking for Christ's return, we will walk towards Christ; if we are distracted, we will take a detour. Be certain that your eyes are focused in the right direction; it is the most important thing we can do in this life!

I remember hearing my father, Ron McKnight, say these words as he would end many of his prayers: I will be careful to give you all of the glory and honor. He did not speak these words as an idiom or idle figure of speech, but they came from deep seeded conviction which ordered his words, thoughts, and actions. Always careful to avoid taking credit for himself, and keen to redirect any praise; my father's words, spoken and lived in sincerity, serve as a bastion of protection against pride and self-righteousness. His life is an open book of Biblical truth and his heart pure and honest. Therefore, it is with his words in mind that I close this book; it is my hope that this book will bring glory and honor to my savior, Jesus, the King of Kings.

> Now to the King eternal, immortal, invisible, to God who alone is wise, be honor and glory forever and ever. Amen. (1 Timothy 1:17, NKJV)

Bibliography

Baxter, I. (2012, July 16). Understanding the Endtime: Endtime Ministries: Irvin Baxter and Dave Robbins. Retrieved July 12, 2020, from https://www.endtime.com/understanding-the-endtime/

Baxter, I. (2012, July 30). 2 Billion to Die in World War 3 - When? Retrieved July 12, 2020, from https://www.endtime.com/blog/2-billion-to-die-in-world-war-3/

Baxter, I. (2015, April 01). Another Jewish Holocaust Ahead: Endtime Ministries: Irvin Baxter and Dave Robbins. Retrieved July 07, 2020, from https://www.endtime.com/another-jewish-holocaust-ahead/

Baxter, I. (2015, April 21). What Do You Mean Born Again?: Endtime Ministries: Irvin Baxter and Dave Robbins. Retrieved June 23, 2020, from https://www.endtime.com/what-do-you-mean-born-again/

Baxter, I. (2015, March 24). Holy Roman Empire Reborn: Endtime Ministries with Irvin Baxter. Retrieved July 12,

2020, from https://www.endtime.com/transcripts/holy-roman-empire-reborn/

Baxter, I. (2015, March 30). The Kingdom of God: Endtime Ministries with Irvin Baxter. Retrieved July 20, 2020, from https://www.endtime.com/transcripts/the-kingdom-of-god/

Baxter, I. (2020, January 29). The "Deal of the Century" Released: Endtime Ministries: End of the Age: Irvin Baxter and Dave Robbins. Retrieved from https://www.endtime.com/end-of-the-age/the-deal-of-the-century-released/

Baxter, I. (2020, June 19). Open Line 387: Endtime Ministries: End of the Age: Irvin Baxter and Dave Robbins. Retrieved June 22, 2020, from https://www.endtime.com/podcast/open-line-387/

Bernard, D. K. (2001). The Oneness of God (Vol. 1). Word Aflame Press.

Brinegar, R., & Robbins, D. (2017, March 2). Time to Build the Third Temple: Endtime Ministries: End of the Age: Irvin Baxter and Dave Robbins. Retrieved June 21, 2020, from https://www.endtime.com/articles-endtime-magazine/time-build-third-temple/

Central Intelligence Agency. (2018, February 01). The World Factbook: India. Retrieved July 21, 2020, from https://www.cia.gov/library/publications/the-world-factbook/geos/in.html

Chapman, G. D. (2015). The 5 Love Languages: The Secret to Love That Lasts. Christian Art.

Donovan, A. (2020, May 04). Antoine Lavoisier. Retrieved June 21, 2020, from https://www.britannica.com/biography/Antoine-Lavoisier

Easton, M. G. (1897). Jehoshaphat, Valley of Definition and Meaning - Bible Dictionary. Retrieved June 21, 2020, from https://www.biblestudytools.com/dictionary/jehoshaphat-valley-of/

Endtime Blog. (2014, April 4). Revelation: The Seven Trumpets and When They Shall Sound. Retrieved June 21, 2020, from https://www.endtime.com/blog/revelation-seven-trumpets-shall-sound/

Endtime Blog. (2018, April 12). Why We Believe in a Post-Tribulation Rapture: Endtime Ministries with Irvin Baxter. Retrieved June 21, 2020, from https://www.endtime.com/blog/why-we-believe-in-a-post-tribulation-rapture/

Endtime Magazine Articles. (2010, May 19). Two Simultaneous Harvests: Endtime Ministries with Irvin Baxter. Retrieved

June 21, 2020, from https://www.endtime.com/articles-endtime-magazine/two-simultaneous-harvests/

Holy Bible: The Christian Standard version. (2017). Holman Bible Publishers.

Holy Bible: The New King James version, containing the Old and New Testaments. (1982). Thomas Nelson Bibles.

Merriam-Webster. (n.d.). Atone. In Merriam-Webster.com dictionary. Retrieved July 5, 2020, from https://www.merriam-webster.com/dictionary/atone

Merriam-Webster. (n.d.). Logo. In Merriam-Webster.com dictionary. Retrieved June 20, 2020, from https://www.merriam-webster.com/dictionary/logo

Purdue Writing Lab. (n.d.). Aristotle's Rhetorical Situation // Purdue Writing Lab. Retrieved June 20, 2020, from http://owl.purdue.edu/owl/general_writing/academic_writing/rhetorical_situation/aristotles_rhetorical_situation.html

Robbins, D. (2020, February 27). Is Bible Prophecy a Fairytale?: Endtime Ministries: End of the Age: Irvin Baxter and Dave Robbins. Retrieved July 11, 2020, from https://www.endtime.com/podcast/is-bible-prophecy-a-fairytale/

Sarna, N., & Faherty, R. (2018, October 02). Old Testament canon, texts, and versions. Retrieved June 21, 2020, from https://www.britannica.com/topic/biblical-literature/Old-Testament-canon-texts-and-versions

Strong, J. (1890). Christos Meaning in Bible - New Testament Greek Lexicon - King James Version. Retrieved June 20, 2020, from https://www.biblestudytools.com/lexicons/greek/kjv/christos.html

Strong, J. (1890). Dibrah Meaning in Bible - Old Testament Hebrew Lexicon - King James Version. Retrieved June 20, 2020, from https://www.biblestudytools.com/lexicons/hebrew/kjv/dibrah.html

Strong, J. (1890). Doxazo Meaning in Bible - New Testament Greek Lexicon - King James Version. Retrieved June 20, 2020, from https://www.biblestudytools.com/lexicons/greek/kjv/doxazo.html

Strong, J. (1890). Eikon Meaning in Bible - New Testament Greek Lexicon - King James Version. Retrieved June 20, 2020, from https://www.biblestudytools.com/lexicons/greek/kjv/eikon.html

Strong, J. (1890). Enistemi Meaning in Bible - New Testament Greek Lexicon - King James Version. Retrieved July 07,

2020, from

https://www.biblestudytools.com/lexicons/greek/kjv/eni
stemi.html

Strong, J. (1890). Logos Meaning in Bible - New Testament
Greek Lexicon - King James Version. Retrieved June 20,
2020, from

https://www.biblestudytools.com/lexicons/greek/kjv/log
os.html

Strong, J. (1890). Mal'ak Meaning in Bible - Old Testament
Hebrew Lexicon - King James Version. Retrieved June 20,
2020, from

https://www.biblestudytools.com/lexicons/hebrew/kjv/
malak.html

Strong, J. (1890). Phaneroo Meaning in Bible - New Testament
Greek Lexicon - King James Version. Retrieved June 20,
2020, from

https://www.biblestudytools.com/lexicons/greek/kjv/ph
aneroo.html

The Editors of Encyclopaedia Britannica. (2018, February 07).
Special relativity. Retrieved June 21, 2020, from
https://www.britannica.com/science/special-relativity

United States Census Bureau. (2010) "U.S. and World
Population Clock." Retrieved July 6, 2020, from
https://www.census.gov/popclock/

Valkanet, R. (2010). Bible Timeline - Old Testament. Retrieved
    June 22, 2020, from
    https://biblehub.com/timeline/old.htm
Zondervan Academic Blog. (2018, January 12). When Was Acts
    Written? Retrieved June 21, 2020, from
    https://zondervanacademic.com/blog/when-was-acts-
    written

About the Author

Jerrod B. McKnight

Jerrod McKnight is a licensed minister with the United Pentecostal Church International and author of the new book Unknown Jesus. With over a decade of experience in healthcare information technology, Jerrod prescribes spiritual cures for eternal health as he writes about Biblical truth in common, everyday language. He holds a Jurisprudence Doctor degree from the Nashville School of Law, but his education began much earlier. From early childhood, his education was not necessarily by choice, but by assimilation. Even though it was not always appreciated, the 'Bible belt of America' provided an excellent environment in which to learn and grow in God's Word. He attributes the bulk of his success in life to the foundation laid through Sunday school, church, prayer meetings, community gatherings, and family events. The principles learned from an early age have proven to be the solid foundation that supports his life and values today.

Made in the USA
Monee, IL
30 March 2021

64102312R00187